History for Teens :

The 19th Century through World War I (1848 - 1918)

Taryn Earley

illustration by Stephen Wisdom

www.openchannelpublishing.com

To Winter, Caelen, Tyler, Masen and Leoh

in the hope it will inspire them to follow their own passions and interests

Content

About the author

Taryn Earley is a historical interpreter, primary school teacher and secondary-level tutor who has developed her own successful style of teaching, working within schools and with the home educated community. As well as classroom teaching, Taryn also makes replica historical costumes and runs hands-on history workshops for schools and groups, aimed at encouraging children to develop a long lasting interest in and love of history.

Taryn has taught 19th century history to teenage students for several years, and composed this work as a resource for her students when no appropriate one could be found.

Preface

History is a subject that I have always been interested in. As a young child, it was my favourite subject. However, as I became a teenager, with different teachers, I began to find the subject boring. The way in which subjects are presented is so important for pupils and can lead to either a love or a hatred. When I had children of my own, I saw them bored by school and disinterested in the subject matter. For them to succeed, their interest needed to be rekindled. I decided that teaching needed to be lively and fun and that being engaged in a subject was the only way to learn. We embarked on several years of home-education where my children soaked up all the exciting experiences provided for them. Now as a teacher, I try to bring that same level of excitement, discovery and enthusiasm into my classroom for my pupils, no matter what the subject is.

As a teacher of 19th century history, preparing students for their examination, I found there to be a lack of comprehensive information to which they had access and no particular text book available which covered the whole syllabus. There seems to be an abundance of material covering the 20th century, but very little on the 19th. In an attempt to remedy the situation, I began to put together weekly hand-outs for my students to use as revision notes. These proved very useful and, over time, have developed into a the book you see before you.

Teachers

This book can be used in one of two ways: either as reading homework and revision after the lesson or, as I have found more useful, as *preparation*, allowing students to gain knowledge and understanding of each topic beforehand, enabling them to engage in in-depth discussion *during* the class.

Suggested discussion questions appear at the end of each chapter or section.

Pupils

This book will provide you with a good basic understanding of life and events worldwide during the 19th century. It is aimed at pupils aged 14-16 years studying for formal exams but, for those aiming higher, or just reading for interest, it is a good starting point and will hopefully inspire further enquiry.

Although this book is predominantly about the 19th century, you will find reference to 18th century events also. Though not essential, some familiarity with some of the major 18th century events, such as the French revolution and the American War of Independence, would be useful, since they often led to those in the 19th century.

The 19th century saw some major eruptions that shaped the world as we know it today, but many of them are not that well known. Despite it being relatively recent history, I find students are often astounded and amazed, and ask why they have never heard of these things before.

I have always found history fascinating, and that stories of real events can be just as exciting and astonishing as those imagined in works of fiction. I also find it interesting how time and time again humans follow the same patterns and make the same mistakes. A knowledge of our past is such an important factor in ensuring that we don't continue repeating these mistakes in the future.

Chapter 1

Industrial development

1.1 The Industrial Revolution

The Industrial Revolution is the name given to changes that took place first in Britain and transformed a farming society into a nation dominated by industry, earning it the nickname 'Workshop of the World'. These changes would ultimately affect every aspect of people's lives. Some benefitted greatly, but a vast majority saw a shocking conversion that could never be reversed.

Agricultural revolution

In the years leading up to the Industrial Revolution, farming changed in Britain. For many centuries, villages had been surrounded by open fields. Villagers had rented strips to grow their own crops, and had kept their animals on common land. Since 1500, landowners had been gradually enclosing their open lands with hedges and ditches, but after 1760 more and more land was enclosed. This previously *common* land was no longer available for local people to use. Instead, farmers worked it for profit.

During the 18th century British farming methods also began to change and slowly became more and more efficient. Farmers were able to produce more food from their land and make larger profits.

In 1701 Jethro Tull invented the seed drill, which drilled holes in the soil, put a seed in each hole, and covered the seed up, in one operation. Previously, seeds had been sown using a 'broadcast' method, which meant that they were simply thrown onto the surface of the earth by hand. The seed drill meant that seeds stood a much better chance at germinating.

In 1730 Viscount Townshend improved methods further by planting in rotation. He realised that different crops removed or returned different nutrients to the soil. By planting turnips periodically, he could not only improve the soil for other crops, but could also use the turnips as cattle food during the winter months and improve his meat too.

The 19th century saw many improvements to farming machinery and a greatly increased amount of food produced. Demand for this food also increased as between 1750 and 1900 Britain saw its population dramatically increase. No one really knows why the population increased so dramatically and so suddenly. It could be linked to better medicine and/or better food, but the main reason seems to be an increase in the number of babies born and surviving. During the 18th century, the proportion of the population who were unmarried decreased. Women tended to marry slightly younger. These changes in marriage may well explain the rise in birth rate and hence the population increase.

With farming becoming more industrialised, fewer people were required to work the land and new employment had to be found. This meant a huge change in lifestyle for many people.

Textile revolution

As well as needing food, the growing population also needed clothing. Until the 17th century, most cloth was made from wool, but now a new cheaper material — cotton — was in high demand and being imported into Britain.

Before the 18th century, all manufacture of cloth was done by workers in their own cottages or small workshops. Spinning was seen as a job for women while weaving was seen as a man's job. Children were also involved in the family business, helping in areas where they were able. As the adults worked at home, someone was always there to look after the children. This situation is often depicted as rather idyllic. People worked in the conditions they lived in, and breaks, meals, and fresh air could be accessed whenever needed. Workers could work at their own pace and take pride in what they did. However, the domestic system did have a number of major weaknesses. In cottage industry, production was very slow. The work could make the air in the home very dusty, and the hours they could work would have been governed by daylight. Also, there was no regular wage, and no money at all if the product was not complete or the worker became sick or injured.

With a growing population, ways of increasing production were needed.

Inventors

In 1733 John Kay invented the 'Flying Shuttle', using his previous knowledge as a weaver to develop his machine. It greatly accelerated the speed at which weaving could be performed by allowing the shuttle carrying the weft to be passed through the warp threads more quickly and over a greater width of cloth. The invention was not, however, appreciated by the weavers who saw it as a threat to their jobs. Kay was persecuted for his idea and in 1753 his house broken into and his constructions damaged and destroyed.

Some manufacturers were quick to use the Flying Shuttle, but Kay saw little reward as they failed to pay him any royalties, and the cost of taking them to court ruined him. He eventually left England and headed to France to try and sell his invention, but failed there also and died in poverty.

In 1765, James Hargreaves invented the 'Spinning Engine', or 'Spinning Jenny', a multi-spool spinning wheel. This machine dramatically reduced the amount of work needed to produce yarn, with a single worker able to work eight spools at once. When he tried to sell his invention, spinners, fearing they would not be able to compete, attacked his home and destroyed his machine. Hargreaves did not apply for a patent for the Spinning Jenny until 1770, by which time many others had copied his idea without paying him any money. Over the years that followed, they made improvements to the machine and increased the number of threads it could spin from eight to eighty. By the time Hargreaves died in 1778, over twenty thousand Spinning Jennies were being used throughout Britain.

Richard Arkwright was born in 1732 and is considered to be the father of Britain's factory system. Originally a wig maker, Arkwright is considered by some to be a great inventor, but others see him as a shrewd entrepreneur and businessman who used other people's inventions for his own purposes. Arkwright lived in a time when patents were rarely used by inventors. He used this to his advantage, making small improvements to the inventions of others and then claiming patents of his own.

Arkwright put his name to the Spinning Frame, which was first put into use in Preston in 1768. Initially horses were used to power the machine, but Arkwright quickly saw that water would be a much more consistent source of power, allowing it to work continuously. The Spinning Frame would need few people to keep it running, but it would need fast-flowing water. A purpose-built building near a river was needed to house the machine. While an engineer was required to run it, everybody else could be unskilled and therefore paid little. Skilled weavers and spinners would not be needed.

In 1769, Arkwright moved to Nottingham where he teamed up with fellow inventor, Jedediah Strutt, and in 1771 established a large water-powered mill at Cromford. The mill was very successful and by 1789 had several hundred employees. The Cromford mill is often referred to as the first factory in the world.

Arkwright's tendency to 'borrow' other people's ideas caught up with him in 1785 when the patent for his spinning frame was withdrawn by the courts. Despite this set-back, he was already established in the cotton market and his importance was recognised by George III, who knighted him. By the time of his death in 1792, Arkwright was a very wealthy man.

Another invention to make a huge difference was Samuel Crompton's 'Spinning Mule'. Crompton had worked as a spinner since childhood and invented a machine to make his own life easier. It combined the good points of the Spinning Frame and the Spinning Jenny, creating a machine that could spin cotton thread better than any other, despite being originally designed to spin muslin.

Unlike Arkwright, Crompton could not afford to take out a patent on his invention. He was to see his machine being used right across the country, without earning him anything. In later years Crompton appealed to the government for a grant for his contribution to industry, which he was awarded.

In 1785 Edmund Cartwright invented the power loom. This was a steam-powered, mechanically operated, version of a normal loom, which combines threads to make cloth. Cartwright did manage to achieve a patent for his machine but did not make much money.

He too ended up applying for a government grant.

The age of factories

The whole idea of factories was to massively change the lives of the people of Britain. Clothing could be made cheaper and faster, putting the cottage industry right out of business. People now had to go to where the machines were to find employment.

Machines needed water to power them, and the Pennine region of Northern England was ideal. Here were rivers to provide a source of natural power. The air was also damp, which helped prevent the cotton thread from drying out and snapping. The port of Liverpool was conveniently near and could be used for importing raw cotton from the southern states of America, and for exporting finished goods.

Life working in a factory was to be a big change for those involved. In the domestic system, workers could set their own hours and enjoy a degree of flexibility. The factory working day was strictly governed and much longer — typically twelve to fourteen hours, plus overtime. Breaks were short and workers could be required to mend or clean their machines during them.

Factories were run for profit; any form of protection cost money, so there were no safety guards on the machines. Safety clothing was also non-existent. Workers simply wore their normal day-to-day clothes, which at this time were often loose and created an obvious danger.

Wages for factory workers were low, and some employers paid their workers in tokens (the 'Truck' system), which could only be spent at the employer's shop, where prices were high. Women were paid less than men, and children less still. For this reason, employers preferred to employ women and children. Many boys were sacked when they reached adulthood and had then to be supported by their wives and children. As well as being cheap to employ, children were small enough to crawl under machinery to tie up broken threads. There were plenty of them in orphanages, so they could be replaced easily when accidents occurred. Orphans from workhouses in the south of England were 'apprenticed' to factory owners, supposedly to learn the textile trade. They worked twelve-hour shifts, sleeping in barracks attached to the factory, in the beds just vacated by children starting the next shift.

Cruel discipline was also common in some factories and women and children were easily bullied by 'strappers'. Reports were made of overseers hanging iron weights around a child's neck, hanging them from the roof in a basket, nailing their ear to the table, or dowsing them in water butts to keep them awake. These were perhaps extreme cases.

Some factory owners introduced a system of fines to help control their workers. Fines were imposed for things like talking or whistling, leaving the room without permission, or having dirt on a machine. It was claimed that some employers altered the time on the factory clocks to make their workers late so that they could fine them for lateness. Some employers even required their overseers to raise a minimum amount each week from fines, encouraging overseers to be harsh and corrupt.

The health of workers was adversely affected by their working conditions. Cotton thread had to be spun in damp, hot conditions. Working in these conditions and then going out into the cold night air at the end of a shift often caused pneumonia. The air in some factories was full of dust, which led to chest and lung diseases, and the loud noise made by the machines damaged workers' hearing. Many children who were forced to stand for long hours, or do heavy lifting, grew up with conditions such as knock-knees and bow legs. Many accidents involving children were also recorded as children were forced to crawl into dangerous, unguarded machinery, often when they were so tired they were falling asleep on their feet.

While many factory owners treated their workers badly and thought they should be grateful to have a job, other factory owners tried to look after their workforce a bit better.

Richard Arkwright had some harsh factory rules (such as those imposing fines for whistling at work, or looking out of the window) but he also built homes for his workforce, funded churches, and provided a basic education for his child workers.

An entrepreneur called Robert Owen bought one of Arkwright's factories in New Lanark, Scotland, where he set about improving the lives of his workforce. He provided decent houses, schools, and a co-operative shop for his workers, where they could buy quality items at wholesale prices. They also enjoyed a shorter working day and better wages than most. No child under ten was allowed to work. He supported the 1819 Factory Act and set up the Grand National Consolidated Trades Union (1834).

John Fielden, was a cotton-mill owner from Todmorden, West Yorkshire. He advocated a minimum wage, and always paid his workers well. Workers in his mill had a sixty-seven-hour week, considerably less than many other mills. He only employed children over the age of nine years old and had a school attached so they could receive a basic education. He supported the unsuccessful Grand Union of Operative Spinners trade union when it was set up and was a supporter of the Ten Hours Movement.

Titus Salt, owned a mill making fabric from alpaca wool, in Bradford, West Yorkshire. He believed that if his workers were happy, then they would work harder. He had a whole village built for his workers, called Saltaire. It had excellent housing, with gas and running water, alms-houses, a hospital, schools, a library, a chapel, a public bathhouse, a washhouse, and parks. He put smoke burners into his factories to reduce pollution, and he put the drive shafts underground to help reduce the noise. He was also a supporter of the Chartist movement. He did, however, employ young children as he believed that families needed the money that they could bring home.

John Wood was another mill owner in Bradford. He provided baths for his workers and only employed children part time, as well as providing a factory school for them. The benefits he provided pushed up the price of his cloth, which left him disadvantaged amongst his competitors.

The Luddites

As life became more and more industrialised, many people blamed the machines for their hardships and longed to return to a world before machines had taken their jobs. During 1811 and 1812, cities in

Northern England saw riots, violence, and machine breaking, by a group calling themselves 'Luddites'. They claimed to be followers of a General Ned Ludd, who is thought to have been a fictional character. The government dealt with these protesters harshly and rewards were offered to anyone willing to reveal their identities. Several men were executed for their part in the Luddite violence.

Iron and steel

With new factories and new machines being designed, the need for iron and steel increased. For many centuries, the British had converted their iron ore to iron and steel by heating the raw material with charcoal, made from trees. The iron industry in Britain had been relatively small and confined to just a few areas of Southern England and Wales where there was plenty of woodland to provide the charcoal needed. By the mid-18th century, however, the nation's timber supply had largely been used up. Iron and steel manufacturers were forced to look elsewhere for fuel. The fuel they found was coal.

When coal is heated in the absence of air it turns into 'coke', which burns at a higher temperature and is a far superior material for the conversion of iron ore. It can be packed more tightly into a blast furnace, allowing the heating of a larger volume of iron. In 1709 Abraham Darby, of Coalbrookdale in Shropshire, invented a coke-fueled blast furnace which increased production. However, the iron was of a quality limited to casting into cooking pots, and not adequate for machinery.

'Cast' iron is simply molten iron poured into a mould. Stronger 'wrought' iron undergoes further work to remove impurities. The metal is repeatedly reheated and hammered into shape, making it more flexible. In 1784, Henry Cort came up with a new idea. He first heated the metal in a furnace, and then used huge rollers to flatten and stretch it. This process led to a yet stronger, and cheaper material.

In the latter part of the 19th century, there was a growing demand for something stronger still. Steel is made by mixing wrought iron with carbon. Although it had been discovered many centuries before, it remained too expensive for widespread use until Henry Bessemer invented a better way of making it in 1856. Bessemer's invention was a container called a 'converter' which could make steel quicker and cheaper by blowing oxygen through molten iron. The oxygen combines chemically with carbon and other impurities and burns them out. This became known as the 'Bessemer Process'.

Iron and steel was in great demand at this time and was used for many things, such as building factories, bridges, machines, ships, and railways, and making cannons, rifles, farming tools, kitchen ranges, bedsteads, and steam engines.

Steam power

Steam engines heat water to create steam power, and had been used in primitive forms for many hundreds of years. Developments in the 18th century saw the real value of the power of steam. The first really successful steam engine was invented by Thomas Newcomen in 1712. It worked by burning coal and using the difference in pressure between the atmosphere and a vacuum formed by condensing steam in a cylinder to drive a piston. It was mainly used for pumping water out of mines.

Scottish engineer James Watt made dramatic improvements in the design of steam engines so that they would be more powerful and burn less coal. By 1781, Watt could create enough power from his engine to turn a water wheel. This was a huge development for factories which now no longer needed to be near a water supply and could be built anywhere in the country. Steam quickly took over from water and James Watt became extremely wealthy.

Coal mining

Before 1700, coal came from mines that were near the surface, where it was relatively easy to get to. Two types of mine existed : the 'drift mine' and the 'bell pit'. Both were small in scale, and their produce was used locally, in homes and industry. Coal was used for domestic heating, and in the manufacture of dyes, fertilisers, explosives, and pesticides. Coal gas was used for lighting.

With the rise of industry and steam power, much more coal was needed. As a result, coal mines ran deeper and deeper, and coal mining became more and more dangerous. Coal shafts could go hundreds of feet into the ground. Once a seam was found, the miners dug horizontally to extract the coal.

Deep underground, miners faced huge dangers. Flooding was a common problem as digging below the water table meant that mines could very quickly fill with water, trapping and drowning miners in the tunnels. Pockets of gas could also be encountered. These could be poisonous, or cause explosions. Miners often worked using open candles, before the safety lamp was invented, which was particularly dangerous. To clear mines of gas — be it explosive or poisonous — a crude system of ventilation was used. To assist this, children, as young as four, called 'trappers', would sit underground opening and shutting trap doors which ran across the shaft. These allowed coal trucks through, but created a draught that could shift a cloud of gas. It was also believed that the system of trap doors might help to stop the blast of an explosion damaging more of the mine.

Pit collapses were also common dangers. The sheer weight of the ground above a dug coal seam was enormous and mines were only held up by wooden beams called 'props'. Even getting to and from the coal was dangerous, as miners were lowered in and lifted out of the shaft at the beginning and end of their shift. Falling out of the 'bucket' meant certain death. Also, coal needed to be lifted out of the mine, and any falling onto a miner, as it was being raised, could cause serious injury.

As well as these dangers, working down the mine was a very tough job. Before any regulations were set, men, women and children all worked in mines. 'Putters' as young as six years old could be found pushing tubs of coal or carrying buckets for the 'hewers'. The hewers worked in really cramped conditions cutting the coal from the seam with pickaxes. The 'hurries', usually women, pulled tubs of coal attached to them with chains. Discipline in the mines could be harsh too. Miners were paid by the tub and if their tub was underweight, they were often not paid. There were fierce fines, and some miners ended a week's work owing the mine owner money.

Very little coal was found in the south of England, but vast amounts were found in the Midlands, the North, Wales, and parts of Scotland. Because coal was so difficult and expensive to move, towns and industries that relied on it were built in and around these regions. Previously, much of Britain's wealth had been found in the South-East. The coal mining industry changed Britain's geography as new wealth was created in mining areas and large towns were built to accommodate the workers.

Changes in legislation and working conditions

When concerns were raised about working conditions in factories and mines, especially for children, reformers began to propose changes to improve them. The first supporters of reform were caring mill owners, many of whom were motivated by their religious beliefs. Several Acts of Parliament were passed covering health, safety, working hours, and how children could be employed :

— 1802 *Health and Morals of Apprentices Act*, proposed by factory owner Robert Peel (not to be confused with his son, Robert Peel, who later became Prime Minister), which stated that all factory rooms should be well ventilated and lime-washed twice a year ; children should be supplied with two sets of clothing ; children aged 9-13 can only work a maximum of 8 hours a day and must be taught reading, writing and arithmetic ; apprentices aged 14-18 can only work a maximum of 12 hours a day ; children under 9 should not work and instead must attend a factory school ; children can only work between the hours of 6am and 9pm ; male and female children must be housed in different sleeping quarters and may not sleep more than two to a bed ; children must have an hour's instruction in Christianity on a Sunday ; factory owners must tend to infectious diseases.

— 1819 *Factory Act*, proposed by Robert Owen, stated that no children under 9 were to work in factories and that children aged 9-16 were only allowed to work a maximum of 12 hours a day or 72 hours per week, with one and a half hours a day for meals.

— 1833 *Althorp's Factory Act*, proposed by Lord Shaftesbury, stated that children aged 9-13 were to work a maximum of 8 hours per day, have an hour's lunch break and must go to school for 2 hours a day ; children aged 14-18 were to work a maximum of 12 hours a day, with a hours lunch break ; no children under 9 were to work in textile factories ; no night work for anybody under the age of 18.

The Sadler Report, 1832, recorded the awful conditions workers faced in textile factories and made many people in authority aware of the need for change. According to this view of factory work, not only men, but women and tiny children did physically monotonous and strenuous work in hot, damp, dusty, and dangerous conditions for long hours and very little pay, under a regime of cruel overseers, punishments, and fines. The author, Michael Sadler, was a committed reformer. Evidence was taken from dozens of workers, but it has however been suggested that Sadler misled witnesses, exaggerated the truth, and only reported extreme cases.

In 1842, Parliament published 'The Mines Report' about the state of coal mining, and its contents shocked the nation. The report informed the public that children under five years of age worked underground as trappers for twelve hours a day, and for just two pennies a day. It also told of older girls carrying baskets of dug coal which were far too heavy for them, causing deformities.

Following these reports, further Acts were passed :

— 1842 *Mines and Collieries Act*, proposed by Robert Peel, banned all women, and children under ten, from working underground in the mines, and anyone under fifteen from operating winding gear.

— 1844 *Graham's Factory Act*, forbad children aged 9-13 from working more than 9 hours a day, with a lunch break, and children aged 14-18 and women more than 12 hours, and required factory owners to wash premises with lime every fourteen months, accidental death to be reported and investigated, and safety guards to be fitted on all machines.

— 1847 *Fielden's Factory Act*, proposed by John Fielden, saw a 10-hour day introduced for those under 18 and for women (excluding silk and lace mills).

— 1878 *Factory and Workshops Act* barred women from working more than 56 hours a week and children under 10 from working at all. It also introduced safety laws, highlighted the need for ventilation, and required set meal times for employees.

All these laws showed that the need for improved conditions was recognised by those in authority, but often these laws proved difficult to enforce. Factory inspectors were easily bribed as they were poorly paid, and there were so few of them that covering all of Britain's factories would have been impossible. Even after this legislation, many children still worked illegally in factories. Many working parents were so desperate for money that they lied about the ages of their children to get them work. Many would not have known their actual age. Since birth certificates were not in use yet, no documentation was available to prove this anyway. Even banning child labour altogether did not eliminate the problem as mothers with young children often had to take them to work with them. Some factory owners were only too happy to let them come to work with their mothers, and made use of this now unpaid labour.

Not everyone was keen on improving working life, and these Acts faced strong opposition.

The famous economist Adam Smith pointed out that children had always been employed in the domestic system, where they were often brutally treated, and suggested that conditions in factories were no worse than in the home. Others argued that workers would only squander the extra time and money they were given in drunkenness and crime, and that harsh discipline was necessary as the previously domestic workers were not used to the needs of the factory and had to be trained.

Many were worried that the cost of implementing the new legislation would ruin the industry, which was a major contributor to the wealth of the country. However, it soon became clear that workers who were well treated worked harder and took pride in their work, *increasing* production.

More leisure time and money led to a happier family life and *less* crime.

Revision

Why did industry develop rapidly during the 19th century?

Why was there increasing demand for iron and steel, coal and textiles, and how was this met?

— an increase in the population led to a need for more food, clothing and employment

— there was an increased need for goods such as farm tools, home goods, weapons, ships, bridges, railways, steam engines, machinery

— large textile mills were built

— a lack of charcoal meant a new fuel was needed

— demand for coal increased with the size of the population and the rise of industry

— larger coal mines were dug

— new methods for creating iron and steel were invented.

How important were technological developments in the development of industry?

— the textile revolution led the way for the industrial revolution

— inventions such as the Flying Shuttle, the Spinning Jenny, the Spinning Frame, the Mule, and the power loom, changed the way people worked and took work away from the skilled

— new forms of power led to the building of factories near their sources, taking manufacture away from cottage industry

— industry became much more organised, with a system of hierarchy

— new types of industry were created.

How were workers affected by the industrial changes and the development of the factory system?

— health problems

— a need to relocate

— harsh working conditions (some factories were worse than others)

— misery, hardship and despair

— long working days set by a clock

— low wages

— safety issues

— a change from working as a family

— factory rules, discipline and fines.

How important were individuals in improving working conditions?

Robert Owen, Titus Salt, Richard Arkwright, Robert Peel and Lord Shaftesbury, all helped make changes that would benefit workers.

How important was legislation in improving working conditions?

1802 : Health and Morals of Apprentices Act

1819 : Factory Act

1832 : The Sadler Report

1833 : Althorp's Factory Act

1842 : Mines and Collieries Act (followed the 1842 Mines Report)

1844 : Graham's Factory Act

1847 : Fielden's Factory Act

1878 : Factory and Workshops Act.

Some questions for you to try

1   Why was there a need for more coal?

2   Why was iron used more often than steel in the first half of the 19th century?

3   'The Bessemer Process was the most important reason for the development of the steel industry between 1850 and 1900.' How far do you agree with this statement?

4   What improvements were there in the manufacture of iron and steel?

5   Why was cotton so important in the textile industry?

6   What were working conditions like in the textile mills?

7   How far had working conditions in mines and factories been improved by 1850?

8   Was the description of Britain as the 'Workshop of the World' justified?

1.2 The improvement of transport

Roads

The new factories depended on coal to fuel their steam engines and iron foundries. As more coal was mined, a better method for transporting it was needed.

The main way of travelling around Britain at the beginning of the 19th century was by road. Many of Britain's roads were in a poor state as they had not been rebuilt or improved since Roman times. As industry grew, attempts were made to build better ones for the increased traffic.

Each Parish had to pay for the repair of their own roads. In some areas, 'turnpike' trusts were set up by groups of landowners and merchants, which became responsible for all repairs and improvements. Parliament gave them permission to charge travellers to generate the money needed. These tolls made transporting goods by road very expensive.

Travel by road was also slow, although some attempts to improve things were made. During the 18th century, coaching inns were built along busy routes where fresh horses were kept and passengers and drivers could refresh themselves. Thanks to these, the time taken to make some journeys was greatly reduced.

For passenger travel, the quickest way was by stagecoach. By 1800, these coaches had seen many improvements, such as narrower wheels, which helped to increase their speed. (From the 1780s coaches began to carry letters, replacing post boys on horseback.) Despite these advances, road transport was still not suitable for carrying coal, as horses pulling carts could not move it in large enough quantities. A new method needed to be found and the best option seemed to be the canal.

Canals

The great expansion of canals started in the 1760s but their history goes back much further than this. For many centuries, merchants had used barges on rivers to move their goods. Between 1650 and 1750, much effort had been put into improving waterways.

The first significant canal in the British Isles was the Newry Canal, built in 1742 in Ireland. It was thirty-five miles long and carried coal to Dublin.

In 1761, the Bridgewater Canal opened in Lancashire. The Duke of Bridgewater owned coal mines on his Lancashire estate, but he had no means of getting his coal to Manchester quickly and cheaply. Eventually he solved the problem by employing engineer James Brindley to build him a canal to connect these two locations. When the canal was opened, people were amazed by Brindley's achievement. He had even built an aqueduct to carry the canal over a river. Bridgewater made a great deal of money, and the price of coal in Manchester halved, thanks to cheaper and faster transportation.

Seeing a lucrative opportunity, many people copied Brindley's design, and in the 1790's 'canal mania' took hold, whereby people invested their money in almost every canal project.

Canals were good at moving fragile goods, such as pottery, and heavy goods, like coal. Although they were still propelled by horse power, barges were faster than carriages. Once a horse got a barge moving, its own momentum would keep it going at a decent pace. By 1802, one hundred and sixty-five canals had been created to carry heavy cargo. By 1840, there were nearly 4,500 miles of canal in Britain. Yet within years their great days were over.

There were many problems. Different builders built differently sized canals so that differently sized barges were needed for each route. Canals had to be perfectly flat or else the water would simply run away. (Where it was not possible to go around hills, Brindley designed locks to raise or lower the barge to the correct water level.) Canals could freeze up in winter, and a hot summer might literally dry them out if they were not topped up with water on a regular basis.

For passenger transport they were inadequate as people could only travel to specific destinations. Despite their advantage over road travel for carrying freight, they still were not fast enough to transport goods such as perishable food. A more efficient method was still needed.

Railways

The earliest railways to exist in Britain were operated in mining towns where wagons would run along a simple track and a pulley system would be used to pull the coal or iron out of the mine. In 1804, a Cornishman, Richard Trevithick, built a steam locomotive engine that could pull freight by rail at Merthyr Tydfil in South Wales. It managed to pull ten tonnes, but, like most first models, it was highly unreliable. If the design could be improved, however, it was clear that railways could carry goods all over Britain. The trouble was, no one knew how to build efficient and fast railways properly, and banks were reluctant to lend money to fund something which might not be successful.

In 1811, John Blenkinsop invented a steam engine which had cogs on one of its wheels. These gripped an extra rail laid down on the normal railway line and gave his engine more grip. In 1813, another steam locomotive, *Puffing Billy*, was built by William Hedley to pull coal wagons at the Wylam Colliery in Northumberland. It was so reliable that it was used for fifty years.

The first major developments can be attributed to George Stephenson. From an early age, George seemed interested in machinery and how it worked. By the time he was fourteen years old, he was working with his father on the new machines at a nearby coal mine.

In 1819, he got the chance to build his first railway at Hetton Colliery.

He was fascinated by steam engines and in 1821 was made engineer for the colliery. The owners decided to build a railway line from Stockton to Darlington so they could move their coal to market more efficiently. Stephenson was given the job of building it.

The Stockton to Darlington railway opened in 1825. It carried coal from several collieries to the port at Stockton. Two locomotives, *The Experiment* and *No. 1*, each pulled twenty-one coal wagons, twenty-five miles, at eight miles per hour. This was unheard of at the time, and soon the line was making large amounts of money. People were sometimes also carried, but purpose-built steam trains did not haul passengers on the line until 1833.

Although just a small railway, the Stockton to Darlington marked the start of some huge changes in Britain. Soon railways would span the country.

The 'Age of the Railway' was beginning.

Feats of engineering

Factories in Manchester and Lancashire that were using the Bridgewater Canal felt that a railway would be a cheaper and more efficient method for them to use too. They applied for an Act of Parliament to build one between the two major north-west cities alongside the canal. George Stephenson was again commissioned to design and build the line, but he was faced with a few problems.

The route he chose had four major obstacles that he had to overcome.

15

Stephenson's planned route cut directly through a housing estate in Edgehill. He was told he could not demolish the houses, so instead, he dug a 2,200-yard tunnel beneath them — the first time something like this had ever been attempted. Just outside Liverpool, he encountered a large mound called Olive Mount. He did not want to go around it, so he ordered his workers to complete a two-mile cutting through solid rock. The next stage of the route meant taking the railway over the River Sankey. A stone viaduct had to be built right across the valley. The last major problem was a twelve-mile marsh just outside Manchester, called Chat Moss. Unable to drain it, Stephenson had to lay a foundation of heather and brushwood on which to build the track.

It took almost six years to finally complete this railway, but when it opened in 1830 it was the most direct route between the two cities and became the first successful passenger line to open in Britain.

To mark the opening of this great railway, on September 30th 1830, a competition was held to design the best engine. The engine would need to be able to pull heavy loads, quickly and over a long distance. The competition took place over several days and ten engines were entered. Each one had to prove its worth by taking part in timed trials. Thousands of people came to watch this exciting event and see which engine won. It was a grand occasion, but there was a terrible accident when a man was knocked down and killed by the winning engine, the *Rocket*, designed by Stephenson's son, Robert.

George Stephenson went on to build many other railways before he died in 1848, and his son was to follow in his footsteps. In 1838, Robert Stephenson completed the London to Birmingham line.

The merchants of Bristol watched the railway building with interest and concern. The new line was bringing much more trade to the port of Liverpool, and the port of Bristol was suffering as a consequence. They decided that the answer was to build their own railway, connecting Bristol with London. Isambard Kingdom Brunel was employed as engineer.

The Great Western Railway was built in stages from 1837, and Brunel impressed the world with his tunnels, bridges and viaducts. The line was finally opened in 1841. Not only could goods and passengers now travel from London to Bristol by rail but, with the addition in 1838 of the SS (Steam Ship) Great Western, the journey could continue all the way to New York.

Objection and regulation

Although those that would benefit from railway expansion looked on with interest and considered how they could make a profit from such an idea, others looked on in horror. Some people worried that the 30mph top speed of trains would cause health problems for passengers. Farmers and landowners did not like the idea of any new railway passing through their land because they believed that the trains would scare animals into giving birth prematurely or dying and that the smoke would destroy crops. Members of the aristocracy were annoyed at the idea because they believed that it would hinder fox hunting. The Duke of Wellington feared that trains might encourage the poor and undesirables in society to come to London and that any trains coming from places such as Bath and Bristol, which had to pass near to Eton School, might disturb pupils. Canal companies obviously felt threatened by railway companies stealing their businesses. Some people just did not like the idea of men and women travelling together in the same train carriage.

Despite all these worries, railway building continued on a massive scale after 1830, and by 1832, one hundred and sixty-six miles of track were open. The building of the railway was also a great boost to industry because of the huge amount of iron and coal that was required to build track and power steam engines.

In 1839, Parliament attempted to regulate the railway industry and set up a railway department at the Board of Trade. However, inspectors responsible for supervising the railway companies complained that regulations were being ignored. William Gladstone, President of the Board of Trade, proposed a new Act of Parliament that would make it possible for the government to take over a private company which had not complied with regulations. The 1844 Railway Act also required each company to operate at least one passenger train a day along the length of their track at the rate of just a penny a mile. Carriages had to have seats and be protected from the weather. The Act made passenger rail travel a real option for many more people and prompted the creation of different classes of travel.

Construction

Many thousands of miles of railway were built, and they transformed Britain. The building of railway lines was very labour intensive and required huge numbers of workers, which was good for the country as it created lots of new jobs. The heavy work was done by men known as 'navvies' (short for navigators). By the mid-19th century, at the height of railway mania, there were a quarter of a million navvies across the country. About 1% of the population was engaged in building railways.

Most of the construction had to be done by hand with only simple tools, such as a pick, a shovel, and a wheelbarrow. The work was hard — an experienced navvy could be expected to move *twenty tonnes* of earth a day. By the standards of the time, they were well paid. However, their pay could take some time to arrive, and many railways paid their navvies right next to a tavern, owned by the railway company, which could thus recoup its money.

Their drinking was well known, and many towns feared the arrival of the navvies. They worked hard and they drank hard. "Going on a randy" was navvy slang for going on a drinking spree that could last several days. Navvies usually lived by the line they were building, in huts provided. Approximately twenty men would share a hut, some sleeping on the floor as that cost them less in rent. The accommodation was temporary: when one railway was finished, they would move on to the next.

The work the navvies did was very dangerous and mortality was high. Those working in tunnels that were being built were especially vulnerable to collapse and explosion. Everything was done in a hurry, and safety procedures were minimal. Getting the job done was considered far more important than employee safety, as there were plenty of men to replace those killed or injured.

British navvies earned a reputation for hard work. Many went on to build railways in continental Europe where it was sometimes claimed that they worked twice as hard as anyone else.

Railways change the world

By 1850 there were more than six and a half *thousand* miles of railway in use. Unlike the canals, the railways now provided comfortable transport for passengers as well as the carriage of freight. They helped businesses move raw materials and goods much more effectively right across the country and, not surprisingly, took away custom from the canals. As well as moving industrial materials, railways also proved useful for transporting other goods which impacted on the way people lived: fresh food could now be carried over greater distances before it perished; inland towns could get fresh fish; newspapers could report nationally; music hall performers and theatrical companies were able to tour the country, and sporting teams could travel to play against each other. The new railways also meant a change in the way people spent their free time. For the first time, people could visit the countryside or the seaside for a day trip. This was the beginning of the modern 'holiday', or 'vacation'.

Railways also changed the way people kept time. For as long as anyone could remember, cities all over the world set their clocks by looking at the sun. Whenever the sun was at its highest, it was noon, but, because the surface of the earth curves, noon for a city further east comes sooner, and for one further west, later. If people were to travel from one side of the country to the other by train, they would need to understand when they were leaving and arriving. In 1840, the railways adopted London Time. In 1880, the rest of England followed. This was the first time that people all over the UK had exactly the same time on their clocks.

Wherever railways were built in the world, time differences became an issue. A Canadian railway engineer called Sir Sandford Fleming, suggested that, as it takes twenty-four hours for the earth to revolve once, it might be a good idea to divide the world into twenty-four time zones. Each would stretch from the North Pole to the South Pole, like a slice of an orange, and are what we use today.

Revision

How significant were improvements to transport in the nineteenth century?

What were the disadvantages of roads and canals in Britain in the early 19th century?

— they were inadequate to meet the growing needs of industrial society

— travelling by road was expensive and slow

— the roads were in a poor state, and someone had to pay for their upkeep

— canals were not direct enough and were difficult to build and maintain

— both relied on horse power, which was neither fast enough nor powerful enough.

Why and how did Britain develop a railway system?

— there was a need to transport coal and other heavy loads

— there was a desire for cheaper travel

— goods needed to be moved faster

— engineers like George Stephenson led the way with new technology.

How significant were the social and economic consequences of the railways?

— MPs were able to travel more quickly between their constituencies and the Houses of Parliament in London

— perishable food could be moved quickly, so things like vegetables and dairy products could reach a market while they were still fresh; food became cheaper

— national newspapers could be delivered; communication became easier

— British time became standardised because trains had to run to a set timetable across the country

— railways became a major employer because people were needed to build, run, and maintain them

— political movements spread around the country because members of organisations such as the Chartists and the Anti-Corn Law League could travel to drum up support (see Chapter 4: *Working-class movements*)

— the transport of heavy materials became much cheaper

— people were able to take short holidays and day trips to the beach

— the government could send soldiers by train to stop political unrest and patrol protests

— Britain began exporting locomotives and train parts

— sporting teams travelled to play against each other and standard rules were written

— people feared the speed of the train and the health problems railways might cause

— canal companies came under threat.

How did conditions for passengers improve during the 19th century?

— travelling became faster, cheaper, more comfortable, and eventually safer

— the Parliamentary Train Act 1844 regulated rail travel.

Some questions for you to try

1   What were the disadvantages of moving goods by road?

2   What were the main problems with moving goods by canal?

3   Why did many canals fall into disuse?

4   Why were there many objections to the building of the railways?

5   How far were conditions for passengers on railways improved after 1830?

6   How much did the growth of industry depend upon developments in transport?

7   'Railways had a greater impact on industry than on the lives of ordinary people.'
   How far do you agree with this statement?

1.3 Urbanisation, and its effects on living conditions

Housing

Industrial development changed where people worked. It demanded that huge numbers of them leave the countryside and move to new towns and cities to find employment. These places were not prepared for such an influx in such a short space of time, and suffered huge problems.

Housing all the new workers was a major difficulty, and new affordable accommodation had to be built very quickly. Often the factory or mill owner would provide the housing for their workers, giving employees little choice as to where they lived or the conditions they had to endure. There were few building regulations. Those that did exist were frequently ignored, leaving builders a free hand to build however they wished, with profit the main motivation. The materials used were often the cheapest a builder could find, and the finished homes were often damp and hazardous. Many areas saw the construction of 'back-to-back' terraced houses. These were built in blocks so that the only part of the building not connected to another house was the front. They were usually small and had very little light as the only place to put doors and windows was on the front of the house. None of these homes contained a bathroom, a toilet, or running water. They typically had no garden, but there would often be a courtyard between each row of terraces. Sanitation and hygiene barely existed and throughout the eighteenth and nineteenth centuries the fear of cholera, typhus, and typhoid was great.

As the houses in these poorer areas had no toilets, communal ones were provided. All the residents of a terrace would share a block of toilets in the courtyard. This could mean dozens of people sharing each one. Any drainage system had to be built out of brick as the technology to create metal pipes was not yet available. Building brick drainage could be expensive. Instead, waste was usually collected in cesspits which had to be emptied. Those living in these areas would not have owned their homes, so it was the responsibility of the landlord to arrange this. They were never too enthusiastic; one cesspit could cost several weeks rent to empty, and many landlords were reluctant to pay. As a result, courtyards could flood with sewage, which might seep into the basements and walls of the badly constructed house. When the cesspit *was* properly emptied, the waste was collected and loaded onto a cart by the 'night soil' men. Local laws dictated that this work be done at night as the stench created was too great to be tolerated during the day. It was the night soil man's job to dispose of waste. Sometimes it was taken to a large open cesspit, sometimes it was used as fertilizer, but often it was dumped into the local river.

Fresh water supplies were difficult to get in the poor areas. With no fresh running water, the best people could hope for was to leave a bucket out to collect rain. Some areas were lucky enough to have access to a well with a pump, but there was always the chance that the well water had been contaminated with sewage from a leaking cesspit. With no bathroom, residents either washed in a tin bath in the home, in water collected from a local well, or simply did not wash at all. Those who lived near a river could use river water, but this is where night soil men emptied their carts, and where general rubbish was dumped; any water collected there would have been horribly polluted.

Joseph Chamberlain

Joseph Chamberlain was a politician who became Mayor of Birmingham in 1873. Chamberlain was very concerned about the conditions in which his citizens were living and wanted to see changes that would benefit working people. He ensured that the people of Birmingham had greater access to water and gas by forcibly purchasing the local gas and water companies and then combining them to create more affordable and reliable service. He also cleared the worse slum areas and had better housing built. By 1890, Birmingham was known as 'the best governed city in the world'. Although Chamberlain made some significant changes, he did see failure. Housing was not built in all the areas he had wanted which ultimately meant that not everyone cleared from the slums found themselves rehoused.

Health

With chronic overcrowding, lack of hygiene, little knowledge of sanitary care, ignorance of what caused disease, and no idea how to effect a cure, cities in the 19th century were not healthy places in which to live. Sickness accounted for many deaths.

One greatly feared disease was cholera, which could spread quickly and with devastating consequences. Britain was hit by outbreaks of cholera on numerous occasions during the 19th century. The cause was simple; sewage was dumped in the rivers, which many people used as their source of drinking water. An attack of cholera was sudden and painful. The disease caused vomiting and diarrhoea, leaving the victim severely dehydrated. Without clean drinking water they would die. It usually affected those in a city's poorer areas, though the rich did not always escape.

Smallpox was also a big threat during the 19th century despite Edward Jenner having created a vaccine against it in 1796. Overcrowded housing in the cities served as a perfect breeding ground for the disease. Many people were unaware of the availability of the vaccine, and so had no protection. Smallpox is spread through saliva or close contact with the victim, causing a fever and a blistery rash on the skin. With the limited medical knowledge of 19th century doctors, it often led to complications such as scarring, loss of eye sight, and even death.

Typhoid fever and typhus were two other feared diseases. Both were fairly common during the 19th century, particularly in cities. Typhoid was caused by infected water and typhus was carried by lice.

One of the greatest killers in the cities was tuberculosis (TB). This attacks its victim's lungs, which attempt to defend themselves by producing wart like nodules called 'tubercles'. These became yellow and spongy and caused coughing fits in the sufferer. TB affected those who were undernourished or who lived in dirty and damp housing. It was caught by breathing in the exhaled sputum of someone already infected. Once again, overcrowding escalated the spread of the disease. It is estimated that TB was responsible for a third of deaths in Britain between 1800 and 1850.

People in the early 19th century really had very little idea about the cause of disease. Microbes were only discovered in 1864 by Louis Pasteur. Until that time, all sorts of theories were put forward. A common belief, which dated back to medieval times, was that disease was spread by a bad smell or an invisible poisonous cloud called a 'miasma'. Industrial cities were certainly plagued by bad smells which doctors saw as proof of this theory. Getting rid of dirt and odour would have helped but magistrates, who could create laws to help clean up the city, rarely did so if only the poor were affected. Those with money lived well away from the areas where the poor lived, and any money spent on improving the workers' conditions would have been seen as wasted.

In 1842, Edwin Chadwick wrote *An Enquiry into the Sanitary Conditions of the Labouring Population of Great Britain* where he reported finding a link between unsanitary conditions and disease, high mortality, and low life expectancy. He had no medical knowledge but his conclusions formed the basis of the 1848 Public Health Act which established a Central Board of Health, funded by taxes. Each local borough became responsible for their drainage, water supplies, waste removal, and paving.

Poor medical knowledge meant that this new organisation was not as successful as it could have been. Still convinced that disease was carried in the smelly air, in 1849 Chadwick persuaded the authorities in London to clean up the sewers in their districts and sweep the filth into the River Thames. Unfortunately, the Thames was London's main source of water and, as a result of Chadwick's idea, an epidemic of cholera followed.

Typhoid swept through the town of Croydon in 1852. The local Board of Health went looking for the smell that had caused the outbreak but found nothing. In fact, sewage had seeped into the town's water supply and contaminated it. It did not occur to the health officials that the water could be the cause, and so the disease continued to spread.

Poverty

From the mid-16th century onward, the authorities in England had become increasingly concerned about the problem of poverty. Until the 19th century, local communities were responsible for their poor and money was raised from the wealthy to help pay for their relief. However, many authorities chose to divide the poor into two categories : those who could not help their situation, and those who were in a position to improve their circumstances but choose not to. Those who it was felt were not doing enough to help themselves were punished rather than given assistance.

In 1834, under The Poor Law Amendment Act, the government introduced a new system to 'help' people who could not support themselves, because of unemployment, old age, or sickness. 'Workhouses' were built across the country to accommodate them. In these, families were split up ; women went to one part of the building, men to another, and children to yet another. Parents had limited access to their children, since it was thought that being poor made you unsuitable to be a parent. People were given a uniform, treated very strictly, and given particularly boring jobs, such as breaking stones, picking oakum, or turning a crank. Workhouse food was basic and monotonous. Conditions were very harsh. Smoking and drinking were never allowed.

Ending up in the workhouse was a great disgrace, but it was always a threat, when people became sick or unemployed, which encouraged them to try to keep their job at any cost. Workhouses were like prisons, and it seemed to many that being poor had become a crime.

Education

In 1750, only wealthy male children had any sort of formal education, attending a public school, such as Eton, Harrow, or Winchester. These were violent places in the 18th century, where boys were taught virtually nothing except some Greek and Latin. Girls were less likely to receive an education. If they did, it would usually be limited to skills considered useful for becoming a wife and running a household.

Standards improved during the 19th century. Students were then given a more balanced education, with science, modern languages, and history also taught, and organised games like rugby and cricket played.

In the early 19th century, the government had almost no involvement in providing education. Politicians thought that schools should be run by private owners, churches, or charities. This changed in 1833 when the State began awarding grants. With this help, new elementary schools were set up for ordinary children. These taught reading, writing and arithmetic. Not everyone who ran such schools were able to read and write themselves, so the standard of teaching was often quite poor. They were still fee-paying, but were present in every community, giving more children access.

In 1844 Parliament passed a law requiring children working in factories to be given six half-days' schooling every week. 'Ragged Schools' were set up to provide basic education for these very poor, frequently orphaned, children. The cost of this privilege was often taken from their wages.

The system changed again in 1870, when Parliament passed Forster's Education Act, which required education to be available all over Britain to children aged five to twelve. Schools sprung up all over the country, but few of them were free. Many families could not afford the 'school's pence' each week. As it was not compulsory to attend school, many children still did not go. They worked and earned money for their family instead.

It was not until 1880 that schooling became compulsory and all children had to receive an education until they were ten years old. Again, this had to be paid for, and so was unpopular. Many struggled to pay the fees, and often found the loss of the child's wage impossible. One man who could see the difficulties caused was the Mayor of Birmingham, Joseph Chamberlain. He campaigned for free public education, independent of the Church.

In 1889 the school leaving age was raised to twelve, but the greatest change was seen in 1891 when the 'school's pence' fee was finally abolished and schools became free. At last, education really was available to all.

Revision

What were the causes of urbanisation, and its effects on living conditions?

Why was there a rapid growth of towns in the 19th century?

- — a rise in population was concentrated in certain areas
- — factories grew, with their need for proximity to a power source and transport
- — more and more people moved to cities to find work
- — new houses had to be built to accommodate the new workers.

Why did the rapid growth of towns lead to insanitary conditions?

 — a shortage of housing led to overcrowding, with each house often shared by two or more families

 — with a lack of facilities, many areas could not cope with the sudden influx of people

 — poor, damp, and crowded housing conditions helped spread disease

 — without proper drainage, sewage would sit in cesspits which might leak or overflow, contaminating the surrounding area

 — a lack of fresh running water made it difficult for people to stay healthy and fight disease.

Why did it take so long to improve conditions in the towns?

 — a lack of medical knowledge and understanding of the problem

 — no fresh water

 — a lack of facilities

 — landlords were reluctant to pay to have cesspits emptied regularly

 — Government and local attitudes did not favour the poor.

Why had there been some improvement in conditions by 1900?

 — greater wealth meant money was spent in previously neglected areas

 — Public Health Acts forced local authorities to take responsibility

 — some vaccines and better medicine had arrived

 — slums had been cleared and better housing built

 — Chamberlain in Birmingham led the way for change

1834 : Poor Law Amendment Act : workhouses reduced unemployment figures

1844 : Ragged Schools gave poor children an education

1856 : the end of the Crimean War allowed problems at home to take priority

1870 : Forster's Education Act made education more widely available

1880 : mandatory schooling meant every child received an education

1891 : the ending of school fees made education affordable for all.

Some questions for you to try

1   What were housing conditions like in British towns during the first half of the 19th century?

2   Why did towns grow so rapidly during the 19th century?

3   What did Edwin Chadwick find in his 1842 report?

4   Why was the Public Health Act of 1848 ineffective?

5   How successful were attempts to improve public health and housing between 1848 and 1900?

6   How far can we thank the work of Joseph Chamberlain for the improved conditions in British towns and cities?

Chapter 2

Working-class movements

2.1 Government in Britain before the 19th century

There were many changes during the Industrial Revolution in the way British people lived and worked, but the way in which Britain was governed had not altered for two hundred years.

In the 17th century, the country had been torn apart by a violent disagreement over who should rule. For a time, things changed dramatically after Cromwell took power, but the Restoration saw many things return to the way they had been before. Wealthy aristocrats owned much of the countryside and, between 1688 and 1832, these landlords also controlled Parliament. There was no real democracy; all women and most men were barred from voting.

In most constituencies, only a small number of wealthy men had the right to vote. Choice, in an election, was also limited. As a Member of Parliament (MP) was not paid, few men were in a position to stand for election. The local landowner tended to put forward and support the candidate he wanted; to stand against him was rarely worthwhile. Bribery was common. There was no privacy for the voter, so it was easy to bully or bribe someone into voting for a certain candidate. Once elected to Parliament, the MP did as he was told by the landowner who had put him there.

The industrial changes of the 18th and early 19th century made the voting system in Britain even more unfair. Although the population had increased drastically, the number of eligible voters remained the same. Several of the new industrial cities, where huge numbers of people lived, had no MP, while many small rural villages had several representatives. Although this appears unfair by our standards today, during the 18th century it seemed acceptable to the gentry because most MPs saw their job as representing property rather than people. Because of this belief, it also seemed sensible to them that only owners of large amounts of land should be eligible to vote.

By the early 19th century an increasing number of people began to see the unfairness of the system. Changes may have occurred sooner, but problems abroad took the focus of government attention away from issues at home. Britain was at war with her American colonies from 1775 to 1783 and with revolutionary France from 1793 to 1815. She also faced an Irish rebellion in 1798. These rebels and revolutionaries fought for greater democracy. As a result, the British government became even more suspicious of any suggestion of change.

During the Industrial Revolution, the lives of ordinary people in England changed dramatically as they found themselves living in poor conditions and working longer hours, for little money and at the mercy of the factory or mine owner. They became more and more discontented with their lives, which worried the government and wealthy industrialists. After all, there were more who were made unhappy than were made rich by the revolution. The fear was that these people might join together in rebellion, as had happened in France in 1789.

2.2 Political and commercial association

Corresponding Societies

In January 1792 a group of four men, including Thomas Hardy, a London shoemaker, began meeting to discuss forming an association of working men in order to campaign for the right to vote. On the 25th January 1792 they held a public meeting on parliamentary reform. Only eight people attended but they decided to form a group called the London Corresponding Society. As well as campaigning for the vote, they planned to create links with other reforming organisations in Britain. Thomas Hardy was appointed treasurer and secretary. The society passed a series of resolutions which were printed on flyers and handed out to the public. A petition was started which, by May 1793, six thousand people had signed. Soon the London Corresponding Society had made contact with several similar associations throughout Northern England.

At the end of 1793, supporters of parliamentary reform in Scotland organised a convention in Edinburgh. The London Corresponding Society sent two delegates to the meeting, Joseph Gerrald and Maurice Maragot, to discuss ideas. The event did not go to plan; the two were arrested, along with the organizing committee, and tried for sedition (creating speeches or organisations aimed at causing insurrection). Several of the men detained, including Gerrald and Maragot, were sentenced to fourteen years transportation.

The reformers were determined not to be beaten and were soon involved in the organising of another convention. When the authorities heard what was happening, Hardy and two others, John

Horne Tooke and John Thelwall, were arrested and charged with high treason. Their trial was held at the Old Bailey in October 1794. The prosecution, led by Lord Eldon, argued that the leaders of the London Corresponding Society wcrc guilty of treason as they organised meetings where people were encouraged to disobey the King and Parliament. However, the prosecution was unable to provide any evidence that Hardy and his codefendants had attempted to do this, and the jury found them 'not guilty'.

This was not the end of the trouble. By 1795 feelings against the King and Parliament had got so bad that stones were thrown at George III as he travelled to Westminster to open parliament. In response, the government quickly passed the Treasonable Practices Act. Under this, anyone found to have brought the King, the Constitution or the Government into contempt could be transported for a period of seven years. The Seditious Meetings Act (otherwise known as the 'Gagging Act') was also passed, and restricted the size of public meetings to just fifty people. It also stated that lecturing and debating halls, where admission was charged and policies discussed, must have a magistrate's licence, which made the organisation of parliamentary reform gatherings extremely difficult.

Despite these acts, small meetings were still held and the Government was still worried. In 1799, Parliament passed the Corresponding Societies Act. This made it illegal for the London Corresponding Society to meet at all, and the organisation came to an end.

William Pitt, the Prime Minister, also decided to take action to prevent rebel leaders from getting the working classes to stand together to force change. The 'Combination Laws' were passed making it illegal for workers to join together to press their employers for shorter hours or more pay. If workers broke this new law they could be sent to prison for up to three months.

The Peterloo Massacre and the Combination Acts

The war with France ended in 1815, but hard times followed for many people. Unemployment was high and bread was very expensive. With public focus now on home issues, many protests against the Government took place. Most of these were peaceful, but in the summer of 1819 one particular protest got out of hand. On 16th August, sixty thousand people gathered at St Peter's Fields in Manchester to hear campaigners appeal for suffrage and political reform. Henry 'Orator' Hunt had just begun speaking when soldiers charged through the crowds to arrest him. Panic broke out; within minutes, around eighteen people were killed and seven hundred injured. The event became known as the 'Peterloo Massacre'.

Discussions and arguments followed about who was to blame. Many people, including some MPs, blamed the soldiers for being too heavy

handed. The Government defended both the magistrates and the soldiers, and decided that the crowd's behaviour caused them to take such drastic action. The Prince Regent even congratulated the magistrates on their action. The result of this incident was that the Government introduced more laws placing even greater restrictions on political freedom.

As expected, many people were very unhappy about all these new laws. A campaign against the Combination Acts was led by a man called Francis Place, who had previously been a member of the London Corresponding Society. He opened his own tailor's shop in Charing Cross Road and used part of his premises as a library for radical books and pamphlets. Place's library soon became a meeting place for reformers. Francis Place held strong views about a working man's right to suffrage (to vote) and the importance of giving children a non-sectarian education (schooling not influenced by religion). He believed these things would lead to a society with better morals and less crime. Place also offered his opinions on the problems of a growing population and in 1822 wrote and published a book entitled *The Principles of Population*. He shocked his readers by suggesting the use of contraception. Despite these views, Place himself fathered fifteen children.

In his attempt to have the Combination Acts repealed, Place collected information and passed it on to radical politicians such as Sir Francis Burdett, John Hobhouse and Joseph Hume so they could promote the cause in Parliament. Between 1822 and 1824, he collected eight volumes of statistics that he believed proved that the Combination Laws should go. He also suggested that their repeal would lead to the end of trade unions. (A trade union is a collection of people whose aim is to retain their jobs and improve their working and living conditions.) Place was successful in his goal and in 1824 the Combination Acts were repealed. He was, however, shocked when he discovered that one of the consequences of this was the *growth* of the trade union movement.

Friendly Societies

As a replacement for the repealed act, the Government introduced the Amending Combination Act (1825). This allowed for the existence of trade unions but banned them from staging protests.

In some areas, people formed 'Friendly Societies' instead. These were different to trade unions but had some functions in common. As members of a Friendly Society, workers paid a subscription, and the society agreed to provide financial support in the event of death or illness. Instead of just paying out benefits, some became militant and began to lobby and petition Parliament for better conditions and better wages.

In February 1834 six farm-hands in Tolpuddle, Dorset, formed a Friendly Society in the hope of increased wages, as the men were being paid less than the average and less than they felt they could survive on. James Frampton, the landowner, was determined to stop any industrial action and reported the group to the Home Secretary, Lord Melbourne. The men were arrested, tried and sentenced to seven years transportation. They became known as the 'Tolpuddle Martyrs', and many people campaigned for their unjust sentence to be overturned. In 1836, five of the six were released, with the support of Lord John Russell, who had recently become the new Home Secretary. The final member, James Hammett, was eventually released in 1837. Only four returned to England.

Trade unions

In February 1834 the Grand National Consolidated Trade Union was formed, thanks to Robert Owen. Owen dreamed of a socialist society, where workers rights were paramount, and hoped that a national union would help this happen. The objectives of the GNCTU were simple; they wished to improve wages and conditions for the working man, and were prepared to strike if necessary. Owen claimed that his union was successful; in the six months it lasted, it gained around half a million members. Many have suggested that this was quite an exaggeration. Sadly, Owen failed to understand or empathise with the suffering of the workers, many of whom preferred militant action to peaceful protest. Many employers also prevented their workers from joining the GNCTU, by refusing to employ them unless they had signed a document renouncing the organisation.

'New Model' trade unions

Alongside the consolidated unions, like the GNCTU, 'New Model' unions were also set up. These differed in that they tended to be restricted to members with a specific *skilled* trade, who were thus relatively well-paid. This allowed the New Model unions to charge fairly high subscription fees. They leaned towards negotiation rather than strike action, which led to them being viewed as more respectable. Because they represented skilled workers, their members were more valuable to their employers and were not as easily replaced as unskilled people. Therefore their ability to negotiate was greater than other unions. Some New Model unions also restricted the number of apprentices allowed to learn a trade in order to keep this advantage. As well as representation, members also received benefits from their union during periods of illness, injury or unemployment.

Chartists

Some progress for unions was seen when the Reform Act was passed in 1832, which extended suffrage, increasing the number of men allowed to vote in England. Many people were disappointed, however, as there were still financial and property restrictions on eligibility. One of these was Francis Place. He joined with John Cleave, Henry Hetherington and William Lovett to form the London Working Men's Association in 1836 and two years later helped to draft the People's Charter that started the Chartist movement.

Chartists wanted six changes made to Parliament :

— a vote for every man over twenty-one years of age, of sound mind, and not undergoing punishment for crime

— the ballot, which would allow voters to cast their vote in secret without fear of being pressured

— no property qualification for Members of Parliament, so that the best man for the job could be put forward for election, regardless of his wealth

— payment for MPs, so ordinary working men could afford to run as candidates

— equal constituencies, meaning each would have the same degree of representation for the same number of electors

— annual parliamentary elections, to help prevent any member getting too powerful or gaining the opportunity to bribe or intimidate voters.

Chartists often fell into two categories. 'Physical-Force Chartists' were happy to use violence to make their point, whereas 'Moral-Force Chartists', like Francis Place, argued strongly against it.

Although extreme violence was rare, people felt so strongly about the issues they were campaigning for, that things sometimes got out of hand. On 4th November 1839, in Newport, hundreds of Physical Force Chartists, mostly ironworkers and miners from the local area, marched through the town, carrying a variety of homemade weapons, towards the Westgate Hotel, where some local Chartists were being held under arrest. When they were refused entry by the guards and special constables, a fight broke out which culminated in shots being fired into the hotel, one of which injured the mayor. As a consequence, the soldiers were ordered to fire at the mob. Twenty-two Chartists were killed and the rest fled.

The Moral-Force Chartists did not fare much better in their methods. In 1839, 1842 and 1848 they presented huge petitions with millions of signatures to Parliament and took part in strike action. Many were arrested and their demands refused. After the third petition had been rejected by the Government in 1848, support for the group declined. Small groups of men continued to meet and argue for the Chartist reforms, but not to the extent that had been previously seen. Some Chartists tried to establish new villages where they could escape the poverty of towns. The first of these was set up near Watford and named O'Connorville, after a famous Chartist leader. Although the houses were affordable, insufficient land was allocated and the scheme did not succeed.

Despite the apparent failure of the Chartists, five out of their six ideas were eventually adopted.

Co-operatives

Another idea that came about during the 19th century was the notion of a 'co-operative' — an organiza-tion set up by a group to benefit its members. During the 1830s, several hundred co-operatives were formed, some more successful than others. Robert Owen (1771–1858) was the man who came up with the idea. As a successful cotton trader, he believed that his business would be more successful with contented workers who enjoyed good working and living conditions and access to education, for both adults and children. He put these ideas into practice in his cotton mills in New Lanark, Scotland. It was here that the first co-operative store was opened, run by the workers, where they could both buy produce at reduced prices and share in the profits. Owen also had the idea of forming 'villages of co-operation', where working people would drag themselves out of poverty by growing their own food and making their own clothes. Such villages would eventually become self-governing.

Although Owen inspired the Co-operative movement, others, such as Dr. William King (1786–1865), took his ideas and made them more practical. King started a monthly magazine called *The Co-operator* which gave advice on running a shop using co-operative principles. He proposed rules, such as having a weekly account audit, having three trustees, and not having meetings in pubs, to avoid the temptation to drink the profits.

The Rochdale Society of Equitable Pioneers was a group of twenty-eight weavers and other artisans from the town of Rochdale, who, faced with poverty, decided to come together and open their own store, selling food they could not otherwise afford. Seeing where other co-operatives struggled, they designed the 'Rochdale Principles' making their society open to all, without prejudice. After four months, they managed to pool together enough capital and on December 21, 1844, they opened their store with a very meagre selection of butter, sugar, flour, oatmeal and a few candles. Within another three months, they had expanded their stock to include tea and tobacco. They became very successful and were soon known for their high-quality goods.

2.3 Industrial unrest

The London match-girls strike

Although things had got a little better by the 1880s, and people were better off than they had been earlier in the 19th century, many were still very unhappy and several famous strikes took place.

The London match-girls strike of 1888 was held by the women and teenage girl workers of the Bryant & May Match Factory in Bow, London. Writer Annie Besant had written a newspaper article in June condemning the way women in factories were treated, referring to it as 'white slavery'. This angered the Bryant & May management who tried to get their workforce to sign a paper contradicting what Besant had written. The women refused. In retaliation, the management dismissed one of them (on some arbitrary pretext). They decided to strike in answer to this, and in protest against a fourteen-hour working day, poor pay, excessive fines and the severe damage to their health caused by working with yellow and white phosphorus.

With huge numbers of workers on strike the factory management backed down and immediately offered to reinstate the sacked worker. It was, however, too little, too late. The women demanded that their other complaints be dealt with also. A group of them met with the management to discuss their demands but were not satisfied. Very soon the whole factory had stopped work. Some strikers visited Annie Besant to ask for her support with their campaign.

Besant was shocked by the upset her article had caused and felt responsible for the fact that so many were now out of work with no means of support. She helped publicise their plight and a strike fund was set up. Several newspapers collected donations from their readers to help the women. Meetings were held by the strikers and Besant spoke at some of them. Charles Bradlaugh MP spoke in Parliament about the situation and a deputation of match women went there to meet with Members. There was so much publicity that the London Trades Council became involved. Eventually, after three weeks of striking, the Bryant & May management offered a new proposal. They agreed that fines, and deductions for the costs of materials and other things, would be abolished, and that in future the women could take any problems they had straight to managers, without having to involve the foremen. They also agreed that meals could be taken in a separate room, where the food would not be contaminated with phosphorus. The women were content with these terms and accepted them.

Despite the strike being over, Besant and several others continued to campaign against the use of the poisonous yellow phosphorus in matches. In 1891, the Salvation Army opened up its own match factory in the Bow district of London, using less toxic red phosphorus and paying better wages. Their aim was to improve the conditions of women and children who worked from home making yellow phosphorus-based matches, after several children died from eating them.

Despite their backing down, the Bryant & May factory had received a lot of bad publicity from the strike and their continued use of yellow phosphorus. In 1901 they announced that their factory would no longer use the material. As early as 1850, the company had been importing and then making red phosphorous matches but found them too expensive, and only competitive when produced using child labour.

The Salvation Army found the same problem; their own matches were initially three times the price of yellow phosphorus-based matches and the factory struggled to compete on price. It finally closed and was taken over by Bryant & May in November 1901. The House of Commons passed an Act in 1908 prohibiting the use of yellow phosphorus in matches after 31st December 1910.

Only a small percentage of unskilled workers were members of trade unions in 1888. The success of the Bryant & May strike encouraged others in Britain to consider forming unions.

The dockers strike

In 1889 the men who worked at the London Docks demanded that their employers provide them with four hours continuous work at a time and a minimum rate of sixpence an hour. As members of the Tea Operatives & General Labourers' Association, the men went on strike. At first, the employers were not worried about this as they felt that the men would only last a short period without pay and would soon be forced to return to work. Ben Tillett, the General Secretary of the union, had been inspired by the achievements of the match girls the previous year and decided to make a stand. He persuaded several socialist friends to get involved and support the men on strike. Organizations such as the Salvation Army and the Labour Church also became involved and raised money for the strikers and their families. Trade unions in Australia even heard of their plight and sent money. After five weeks the employers realised that the men were not weakening and accepted defeat. They agreed to all the men's main demands. After such a successful action, the dockers formed a new General Labourers' Union and Ben Tillett was elected General Secretary. Thousands of unskilled workers joined it.

These strikes were real milestones in pursuit of rights for working people and showed unskilled workers that they too could demand better conditions.

Revision

How successful were 19th century working-class movements?

What attempts were made to organise the working class?

— early associations, such as the London Corresponding Society

— trade clubs

— Friendly Societies

— Francis Place campaigned against the Combinations Acts

— the Grand National Consolidated Trade Union

— the Chartists

— New Model Unions

— the Co-operative movement.

Why were working-class movements generally weak in the first half of the 19ᵗʰ century?

    — the Combination Acts (1799/1800)

    — hard examples made of those who tried to make changes

    — the law was not favourable to them.

How successful were the courts and Parliament in limiting the power of the union?

1795 : Treasonable Practices Act

1795 : Seditious Meetings Act

1799 : Combination Laws

1799 : Corresponding Societies Act

1825 : Amending Combination Act.

How different was 'New Unionism' from 'New Model' unions?

    — New Model Unions were for individual trades for those who were highly skilled

    — New Unionism brought unions for unskilled workers inspired by strikes such as those by the London match girls and the London dockers.

Some questions for you to try

1   Describe the work of Friendly societies.

2   Why were working-class movements generally weak in the first half of the 19ᵗʰ century?

3   How successful were unions in the second half of the 19ᵗʰ century?
    Explain your answer.

4   What were the aims of the Grand National Consolidated Trades Union (GNCTU)?

5   Explain why the Grand National Consolidated Trades Union (GNCTU) collapsed.

6   How far was the failure of the Chartist Movement due to the use of physical force?
    Explain your answer.

7 Why did trade unions for the unskilled grow after 1870?

8 'The power of the trade unions was reduced in the period 1865–1913.'
How far do you agree with this statement? Explain your answer

9 Who were the Tolpuddle Martyrs?

10 Describe the dockers' strike of 1889.

11 Why did the number of trade unionists grow significantly between 1875 and 1914?

12 How successful had trade unions been by 1914? Explain your answer.

13 What was the Co-operative movement?

Chapter 3

The European revolutions of 1848

In 1848, economic depression had spread throughout Europe and many were faced with unemployment, brought on by recent industrial development. A poor grain harvest and 'blight' in the potato crop had caused a food shortage, leading to high prices. A poor railway system prevented help getting to those who needed it most. Any peasant rebellion or protest was dealt with harshly. People throughout Europe were unhappy and wanted change. More and more were turning towards radical political ideas in the hope of improving their situation.

Great changes over the previous century influenced the way they saw things. The wars in America, and its colonists' declaration of independence from British rule, had opened their eyes to new possibilities. Events in France had highlighted the power that could be seized by the working classes.

3.1 Revolution in France

A brief history

At the end of the 18th century, Louis XVI sat on the throne of France, with his wife Marie Antoinette, and believed he had a divine right to rule. They lived a luxurious life, as did the rest of the aristocracy.

France at this time comprised three 'estates': the nobility, the religious leadership and everyone else. 'Everyone else' suffered and paid high taxes, while the King, the aristocrats and the church leaders made all the rules and lived well. By 1789 the people had had enough. A revolution took place resulting in the execution of the King and Queen.

A man named Robespierre took over the running of the country, creating the 'First Republic'. This soon became known as the 'Reign of Terror' as he beheaded everyone who failed to agree with him, or do as they were told. Once again the population rose up, and Robespierre too lost his head.

The people of France decided it was time to *elect* a leader. The man they elected was a war hero called Napoleon Bonaparte. Sadly, it was not long before he claimed god-like status, invaded neighbouring countries and was sitting as head of a French empire, refusing to give up his crown.

This time it was up to the rest of Europe to sort him out. He was sent into exile on the small island of Elba in 1812, and the brother of the guillotined king was crowned Louis XVIII instead. (Louis XVII, son of Louis XVI, had died in jail.) He proved no better than his brother, and the people of France became unhappy again. A boat full of his own soldiers sailed to Elba to rescue Napoleon and bring him back to the mainland, where he was received with open arms. Louis XVIII fled.

The return of Napoleon to the throne antagonised neighbouring nations. Fighting broke out again between France and the rest of Europe. After the Battle of Waterloo in 1815, Napoleon was again exiled, this time to the even more remote island of St. Helena, where he died two years later.

It was decided to put Louis XVIII back in charge, followed a few years later by his younger brother Charles X, who was worse than either of his brothers. He lived an extravagant lifestyle, not caring about the people, and even took control of the press, so that no one could say anything against him.

Another uprising took place in 1830, known as the 'Three Glorious Days'. The people protested against the king, barricades were put up and the red, white and blue flag of the revolution was flown. With this overwhelming lack of support, Charles too was forced to flee the country.

Once again France had to decide how the country would be run and Louis Philippe the 'Citizen King' was put in charge. He was intended to begin a new monarchy which listened to the wishes of the people, without the power of the previous Bourbon kings.

His reign was known as the 'July Monarchy', though he ruled for eighteen years.

France in 1848

By 1848, although Louis Phillipe was supposed to be a new kind of king, answerable to the citizens, it was not really working. Only wealthy men were allowed to vote, meaning that the majority still had no say in how the country was run. With no means of improving their situation, many could see little difference between the new monarchy and the old.

All the time Louis Phillipe reigned, those who wanted a republic — where the head of state is elected — complained about the dangers of having a king. Extreme revolutionaries even tried to assassinate Louis Phillipe, by planting a gunpowder bomb on the street where his official parade was to pass. The bomb exploded, killing courtiers and soldiers, but none of the royal family were seriously injured.

The French middle class watched changes in Britain with interest. The 1832 Reform Act had given more people suffrage. While the working class in France were slightly better off than its English counterpart, unemployment had forced many skilled people into a lower social order, known as the 'proletariat'. The only real law that benefitted ordinary people was a law passed in 1841 banning the use of child labour under eight years old during the day and under thirteen at night. However, this law was not always obeyed.

Having limited say, and because political gatherings and demonstrations were banned, activists began holding banquets. These 'Campagne des Banquets' provided a legal way for people to meet and discuss their views on government. Between July 1847 and February 1848, more than seventy such events were held throughout Paris, where people discussed their political complaints and toasted their principles. In January 1848 the French government, under Louis Phillipe, banned even this sort of meeting. People were furious and revolted against their so-called Citizen King. Barricades were erected and fighting broke out between citizens and municipal guards. Prime Minister Guizot, seeing another revolution on its way, resigned on the 23rd of February. Upon hearing this news, a large crowd gathered outside the Ministry of Foreign Affairs. An officer ordered the crowd not to pass, but the people in front were pushed forward by those behind them. The officer ordered his men to fix bayonets, probably wishing to avoid shooting. However, in what is thought to be an accident, a soldier discharged his musket, which resulted in the rest of the soldiers firing into the crowd. Fifty-two were killed.

The people became even more angry. Like previous powers, their king was trying to use force against them to get what he wanted. Trees were felled for barricades and fires were lit. They stormed the gates and entered the Palace of Tuileries. Crowds rampaged through the building, smashing royal dishes, vandalising the furniture, and taking it in turns to sit on the royal throne. Louis Philippe, realised that his reign was over. Terrified for his life, he jumped into a horse-drawn carriage and fled to England. When he was stopped and asked his name, he replied 'Mr. Smith'.

He escaped Paris on the 24th February. Many rejoiced at this, but many also worried about the violent way in which events had taken place. There was a fear that the events of 1789 were repeating themselves, and that the same problems that had arisen then would arise again.

A new provisional government was formed, known as the 'Second Republic'. Two major goals were universal suffrage and unemployment relief. Universal male suffrage was granted on March 2nd but, as in all other European nations, women were still denied the right to vote. Help for the unemployed was attempted through the creation of 'National Workshops', which guaranteed French citizens the 'right to work'. By May 1848 National Workshops were employing a hundred thousand people. Laws regarding freedom of speech were also relaxed and newspapers sprung up all over France.

While the poor rejoiced at these changes, many wealthy Parisians protested. They left Paris and took their businesses with them, leaving the city in a state of poverty. After just a month, it looked as though this government would also fail. The National Workshops had brought employment to Paris, but the scheme was poorly thought out and there was very little for the workers to actually do. The population of Paris ballooned as more and more job seekers arrived — more than the scheme could provide for. By May the chairman of the provisional government, Jacques-Charles Dupont de l'Eure, was replaced with an 'executive commission' — a body acting as Head of State, with five co-presidents.

The new government set out to establish a stronger economy and provide financial support for the National Workshops. New taxes were levied, falling on the gentry, peasants, and small farmers. The intention was that the money raised with these taxes would pay for the National Workshops in the cities. At this time in France, the majority of the population lived in the country and worked the land. They did not like the idea of paying more taxes to benefit unemployed people in the city. The new taxes created a split between those who lived in the city and those who lived in the country, and were widely ignored. With a lack of funds, the National Workshops were closed on June 21st.

While those who had resented supporting the workshops celebrated, the people of Paris, who had been relying on them, were furious. Between the 23rd and 25th of June, the city saw yet another revolt — the 'June Days Uprising'. The army was called upon to break up the blockades, turning the people of France against each other, once again. Over a thousand were killed in three days; thousands more were sent to prison.

It was clear that the government was once again failing to meet the needs of the people, so it was decided that they should elect a new president to head the National Assembly. Louis-Napoleon Bonaparte, the nephew of the first French emperor, was elected in December. There were several more suitable and experienced candidates, but it seems that the population felt more at ease with a familiar name, and the possibility of dictatorship, than with continual uprisings and revolution.

Louis-Napoleon was sworn in as President, but things did not run smoothly. He could not convince the elected assembly to do what he wanted. When his four years were up, they refused to let him run for president a second time. Louis-Napoleon was not happy. On 2nd December 1851, he staged a military coup, arrested opposition leaders, and announced changes to the constitution, which he had helped to write. These took power away from the assembly, gave it to the president and made Louis-Napoleon that president for ten more years. A majority of the French people voted in favour of these changes. A year later he declared himself Napoleon III, Emperor of France.

The Second Republic had lasted only five years. Now, the Second Empire had begun.

Napoleon III knew he needed strong alliances in order to expand his empire. He travelled to Great Britain and promised Queen Victoria that he would help the British fight the Crimean War against Russia. (For once, Britain and France would be on the same side.) This was a success. Fourteen years after victory in the Crimea, the Emperor of France, feeling unbeatable, declared war on Prussia. He had worked hard to make the French army strong but failed to appreciate how quickly his new enemy would react. Prussian forces stormed into France before the French could prepare for battle. Louis-Napoleon was ill with kidney stones, but he rode out to meet the invaders.

Things did not go well for the French. Their Emperor quickly realised that his army was outmatched and certain to lose. He threw himself into the centre of the fighting, but his health was deteriorating and he was captured along with thousands of his soldiers.

Messengers took the news to Paris, where the people *celebrated*. France could return to democracy. The Second Empire had ended and the Third Republic could begin. Its leaders made peace with Prussia. Napoleon III was released and fled to England, where he hoped to gather a new army and reclaim his throne. Instead he died during surgery a few years later, without ever returning to France.

3.2 Revolution in Austria

The Austrian Empire was very large in 1848 and covered many areas, including Austria and Hungary as well as parts of what are today Croatia, the Czech Republic, Italy, Poland, Romania, Serbia, Slovakia, Slovenia and Ukraine. It was ruled by the Austrian Emperor, although Hungary had its own 'Diet' — a local government. The empire comprised people of many different ethnic groups, each speaking its own language and dominating its home region. Austria itself contained mainly Germans, while

in Hungary the majority were native Magyars. Czechs were the largest ethnic group in Bohemia. Most of the remaining population was made up of a variety of Slavs. The capital was Vienna, a leading European cultural centre, full of artists, composers, writers and intellectuals.

Klemens Wenzel von Metternich was the chancellor of the Austrian Empire. He leaned towards the idea of equality and tried to form a parliament where ethnic diversity was represented. However, he was unable to fully implement his ambition as Emperor Ferdinand, of the House of Hapsburg, had ultimate control. Emperor Ferdinand was King of Hungary and the son of Holy Roman Emperor Francis II and his wife Maria Theresa (who was also his first cousin). As a result of much inbreeding, Ferdinand suffered from a number of genetic problems, including epilepsy, neurological problems, a speech impediment and an unusually large head. It was believed that he was also unable to have children. Like his father, Ferdinand was all-powerful; the Diet had not met since 1811.

In 1815 the Austrian Empire had taken part in the Vienna Congress, where European leaders had met to arrange a treaty at the end of the Napoleonic Wars. There, they had arranged the 'Concert of Europe', where borders were decided, which could not be altered without the agreement of the other countries. The Quadruple Alliance, between Austria, Prussia, Russia and Britain, which had been responsible for bringing down Napoleon and the French empire, made all the decisions. Austria had held quite a powerful seat at this meeting and, as an outcome, had gained control over more land.

During this period in Hungary, the nobles paid no taxes and were the only ones able to vote. By 1825 the population, hearing of the changes in France, started calling for some of their own. The Diet met to discuss the issue but progress was slow, because the nobles objected and insisted on keeping their privileges. One change that *was* agreed was the introduction of Hungarian as one of the official languages of the country, instead of the former Latin.

Over the years leading up to 1848, the various ethnic groups in Austria became increasingly nationalist, and longed to gain their independence. Maintaining the Concert of Europe was costing the Austrian Empire a lot of money, as soldiers were constantly needed to maintain the borders. As in the rest of Europe, the economy was not doing well. There was unhappiness among the working classes over money, taxes and religion. Metternich had worked for years to hold the Empire together and keep the people happy but, as 1848 neared, the already conservative institution, fearing political uprising, banned university activities and fraternities, and abolished the freedom of the press. This led to underground newspapers and pamphlets, produced by students and liberals wanting change.

In February 1848, hearing that the French had driven out Louis Phillipe and gained control of France, the people of the Austrian Empire wanted the same liberation in their own countries. Just a month later, a radical Magyar group, led by Louis Kossuth, began to make speeches demanding independence for Hungary. These were published in Vienna, where they became a sensation and soon started an uprising. Metternich, who had been closely watching events throughout Europe, became worried. Fearful that Austria would follow France's lead, he decided to flee, and quickly left Vienna. The situation was probably not as bad as he thought, but once news got out that he had left, the Austrian revolutionaries felt they had the upper hand.

Riots broke out in Hungary on March 15th when revolutionaries and students stormed the Buda fortress to release political prisoners. The next day saw demands for a new national government; Count Louis Batthyany became chairman and Louis Kossuth minister of finance. The Czechs, and numerous Austrian-controlled Italian populations, followed the Magyars lead.

Under such pressure, Emperor Ferdinand reluctantly signed a reform package. Hungary would remain part of the Empire, but the Emperor's power would be reduced. These 'March Laws' (sometimes called the 'April Laws') created independent Hungarian ministries of defence and finance, which claimed the right to issue their own currency, through their own bank. Under these new laws, nobles lost their privileges and began to pay taxes. Serfdom ended, and some peasants were able to buy land. Freedom of the press was granted, along with the right to meet for political reasons. A Hungarian national guard was created, and Transylvania was brought under Hungarian rule.

The Czech movement in Bohemia soon received the same status, and the Italian states of Milan and Lombardy rose against Austrian occupation.

Not everyone was happy, though. The non-Magyar groups in Hungary feared nationalism — when a single race would dominate within a country — and were disturbed that Transylvania had been taken over. The Vienna government saw this weakness and used it. They enlisted these minorities in an attempt to overthrow the new Hungarian government.

In June 1848, in Prague, Bohemia, a group of Slavic nationalists held a conference to discuss independence from the Austrian Empire. The meeting was badly organised and did not go to plan. Fighting broke out in the streets and Emperor Ferdinand used his army to restore order and end the meeting. He also sent his forces against the rebellious Italian states of Lombardy and Milan, and soon brought them back into line. By summer the revolution seemed to be losing momentum and the Austrians ordered the Hungarian government to resign. That order was ignored.

In September, the newly appointed Goverer of Croatia, Josip Jelacic, led an army into Hungary and forced Batthyany to resign, but Kossuth's guard retaliated and defeated them. A committee of national defence, led by Kossuth, took control instead and established a Hungarian army, issuing paper money to fund it. Louis Kossuth started a movement to make Magyar the official language, instead of Hungarian, even though only half of the population spoke it. The Serbo-Croatians, who had their own language, rebelled and asked the Emperor for help.

On October 6th Ferdinand prepared to send troops into Hungary to bring it back into line. However, as they were due to leave Vienna, people who supported the Hungarian revolution tried to prevent the soldiers from leaving. Soon violent street battles were taking place, and the Austrian Minister for War, Count Baillet von Latour, was lynched by the crowd. The following day, the Emperor and his court fled to the area now known as the Czech Republic. Under the protection of Alfred I, they laid plans for bringing Vienna back under their control.

The combined Austrian and Croatian armies attacked the rebels in Vienna on October 26th. By the 31st they had stormed the city. The rebel defence was led by a Polish General, Jozef Bem. As things started to look bad, Bem fled the city, while the rest of the leaders were rounded up and executed. With Vienna back under control, Prince Felix von Schwarzenberg became the new chancellor.

Emperor Ferdinand had not proved himself to be a strong leader. While the revolutions had been taking place, his mental state had deteriorated. He was declared unfit to rule and persuaded by Prince Felix to abdicate, on December 2nd, leaving his nephew, Franz Joseph, in power.

At this time, Hungary was still independent, and led by Louis Kossuth. Franz Joseph declared that, as he had not been the one to sign the March/April Laws, giving Hungary its freedom, he did not feel compelled to respect them. Instead, he set about bringing the empire back under control. With the help of the Russians in 1849, Franz Joseph invaded Hungary and forced its surrender, on August 13th. Kossuth escaped capture, but many leading figures in the revolt were rounded up and executed. Several women involved were publicly flogged. Hungary's right to make its own laws were removed and the Emperor took full control.

The revolutions in the Austrian Empire had failed.

This failure may have been due to the structure of Austrian society. Unlike Britain and France, Austria had no well-developed middle class, which left no powerful support for revolution, particularly in Vienna. Many peasants and soldiers did not understand the vision of Kossuth. They remained loyal to the Emperor and helped put down revolution.

With the Emperor back in charge, Hungary became more repressive than ever.

While other European countries saw progress towards liberty through revolution in 1848, the Austrian Empire outlawed political gatherings and any display of nationality or support for the revolutionaries, including the wearing of Kossuth-style beards.

3.3 Revolution in Italy

In 1848, there *was* no Italy. Italians lived on the Italian Peninsula, but numerous distinct states occupied the area, each with their own laws, borders and rulers. The largest of these were :

— Tuscany

— the Papal states

— the Kingdom of Piedmont-Sardinia

— the Kingdom of the Two Sicilies (a.k.a. the Kingdom of Naples)

— the Kingdom of Lombardy-Venetia (including both Milan and Venice).

The Kingdom of the Two Sicilies had been ruled by the Bourbon kings, and that of Lombardy-Venetia by Austria, since the 1815 Concert of Europe/ Congress of Vienna. All states were absolute monarchies, but were generally kinder to the poor and to women than other European countries at the time: in some, the poor could own their land; in the north, women could take part in public affairs.

During the 19th century, many of the people who lived in these Italian states began to believe that 'Italy' should be a united nation, free from Austrian rule. They began meeting, in secret societies, to discuss their ideas. Although all the different societies wanted to unite the states into one nation, they could not agree on the *kind* of nation. Some wanted a republic and to vote for a president, while others wanted a union under the leadership of the Pope — the head of the Roman Catholic Church, who lived in Rome. Others wanted the country to be a monarchy, ruled by a king, and even suggested that the King of Piedmont-Sardinia would be the best man for the job.

Despite these different ideas, there was one point they all agree on. No one wanted Austria ruling any Italian state. In 1831, one secret society, 'The Carbonaria', united all the others in a revolt against Austrian rule. The Austrians responded by sending soldiers to break up the rebellion. Hundreds of society members were arrested. The ringleaders were sentenced to be hanged or shot. One of them, Giuseppe Mazzini, escaped. He was horrified to see the other leaders killed, but it made him more determined. He formed a new society called 'Young Italy'. Every member had to be under forty years old and prepared to use violence.

The Young Italians knew that two hundred years earlier, in the days of the Renaissance, the Italian states, although separate, had been powerful and free from foreign influence. They hoped to make them free and powerful once more, but this time united in a single Italian republic. Their movement became known as the Risorgimento (resurgence).

Mazzini was an intimidating individual who claimed that God wanted Italy to be free. He always wore black, and taught his followers that it was right to assassinate tyrannical leaders. In fear, Austria declared that being a member of the 'Young Italians' was a crime punishable by death. Despite this threat, the society continued to grow. New members included a sailor, Giuseppe Garibaldi, who soon became Mazzini's right hand man.

Throughout the Italian states, unhappiness and unrest were growing. On the 12th of January 1848, the people of Palermo, Sicily, who were still upset by the outcome of the 1815 Concert of Europe, started to demand change. They were well organised; posters and notices were handed out three days before the date they planned to revolt — the birthday of Ferdinand II, ruler of the Two Sicilies. The protest had lots of support, including that of the nobles. They declared independence from the Bourbon king and brought back the pre-1812 constitution, which allowed some democracy and the election of a parliament. All of Sicily, except the city of Messina, followed the re-established constitution. It was also suggested then that a confederation of all Italian states should be created.

The uprising in Sicily was to be the first of many that year.

In Milan, fed up with Austrian rule, they planned to upset the Austrian treasury. By stopping smoking and playing the lottery, they denied the Austrians the taxes involved. As people gathered in the streets in support of this plan, Austrian soldiers, worried by the demonstration, shot into the crowd and killed sixty-one people. In retaliation, citizens armed themselves and set up barricades. Violence filled the city from the 18th to the 22nd of March, which became known as 'The Five Days of Milan'. By the end, Austrian soldiers were forced to leave, and revolutionary leaders pledged allegiance to the King of Piedmont-Sardinia, Charles Albert of Savoy.

Seeing this, the people of Trento raised the tricolour flag (demonstrating that they were in favour of a republic), destroyed the office of finance, marched to the city hall and insisted that a message be sent to Vienna, demanding that Austria withdraw from all Italian lands. The following day, they created a national guard, and appealed to other Italian citizens to follow their example. Venice followed suit and declared itself an independent republic.

Charles Albert of Savoy saw all this as a great opportunity to get rid of the Austrians and take more land for himself. By March 24th, his Piedmont army had marched into Lombardy to support the rebels. The Austrian commander there retreated to a group of fortresses. After this move, the Pope, Leopold, Grand Duke of Tuscany, and the King of the Two Sicilies were all pressed by their people to send troops against Austria as well.

Initially, they seemed to form a united front, but Charles Albert was only really interested in claiming cities for his own kingdom, and the Pope soon changed his mind. Pope Pius IX decided that he could not get involved in a war between two states which were both Catholic, and, in May, withdrew his troops. Without the support of the Church, the other Italian leaders quickly followed suit.

This left the fighting between Piedmont-Sardinia and Austria, which was winning. The rebels retreated to Milan. There, the Austrians gave permission for civilians not involved to leave; half the population fled. Charles Albert decided to abandon the city and sign a treaty with the Austrians, agreeing a return to the old borders.

Although the war between Austria and Piedmont-Sardinia had ended by August, Venice was still holding its ground and other states slowly began to join the fight again. In Rome, the people were unhappy and the Prime Minister, Pellegrino Rossi, was assassinated. As things became more and more violent, the Pope fled from Rome to Naples, where he was soon joined by the fleeing Grand Duke of Tuscany, Leopold II.

With Rome free from the Pope, Garibaldi and Mazzini set about building a 'Rome of the People', getting rid of taxes and creating work for the unemployed. A Roman Republic was declared. Mazzini inspired his people to build a better nation, while he lived in cheap housing, led a frugal lifestyle and gave most of his money to charity. He took some of the large amounts of land owned by the Church and gave it to the poor; made reforms to the prison system, and in asylums; granted freedom of the press; set up secular schools, free from church interference, but decided to avoid the 'right to work' idea that had recently failed in France. Despite all Mazzini's hard work, the new republic faced inflation and other financial problems caused by the cost of sending troops to help defend Piedmont-Sardinia against Austria.

The Pope, hiding in Naples, was determined to get Rome back, and sent out messages to Roman Catholics throughout Europe begging for their help to drive out the 'Young Italians'. In France, Louis Napoleon was President and he thought helping the Pope would encourage loyalty from the Catholics in France. Soon French soldiers were heading towards the Italian Peninsula. The army of 'Young Italian' volunteers, commanded by Giuseppe Garibaldi, attempted to hold them off. They even sent them back out to sea, but the French soldiers were well-trained, unlike the revolutionaries, and soon landed again. For three weeks Garibaldi's men prevented them from reaching the city of Rome, but the French were just too strong; finally, the Young Italians had to give up and run. Mazzini escaped capture and fled to London. Garibaldi went to the United States.

The revolution had failed in Rome. Things were not looking much better in Venice. The Austrians had blockaded the city, cutting off supplies. Faced with a fear of starvation, a well-equipped enemy, bombing by hot-air balloons overhead and an outbreak of cholera, the rebels surrendered.

Austria reclaimed the Italian states and the Pope returned to Rome, once the French had left. Many people were publicly flogged for their involvement in the revolution, and hundreds were executed for owning firearms. Wealthier revolutionaries paid fines or had their property confiscated. Sicily held out the longest, but the Bourbon army were able to take back the island on May 15th 1849 by landing in Messina. Revolutionary leaders there fled to Malta.

The 1848 revolution in Italy had failed.

3.4 Revolution in Germany

In 1848, there *was* no Germany. Ever since the Thirty-Years War and the Peace of Westphalia in 1648, which had broken Germany up, its inhabitants had not thought of themselves as German, but as citizens of the fragment in which they lived. There were hundreds of little German states, all ruled by independent leaders, mostly princes. One of those states was Prussia.

In 1806 Prussia had suffered defeat by Napoleon Bonaparte. It lost land, had to pay indemnity and was forced to reduce its army. In the following years focus fell on rebuilding its status. Prussia improved its educational system and overhauled its army. During this period there was a growing sense of German identity. Germans spoke a common language, shared cultural traditions and all hated the French, but they still did not see themselves forming one nation.

At the end of the Napoleonic war in 1815, both Prussia and the German state of Austria profited from the Concert of Europe. Prussia gained part of Saxony, part of Poland, the Rhineland, Westphalia and Pomerania, doubling its population despite losing territory to Russia. Austria gained the Italian state of Lombardy-Venetia, among other things. A German Confederation of thirty-nine states was also created from the three hundred and sixty previous ones and put under the leadership of the Austrian Emperor, with part of Prussia included. This confederation was not concerned with uniting Germany, nor did the individual rulers of the thirty-nine states wish to lose any power; they merely wanted to join forces in a time of conflict.

Klemens von Metternich, Chancellor of Austria, was particularly keen not to see a united Germany. He feared that there might be another revolution and the monarchy overthrown. As most of the other leaders felt the same way, he was able to use the Confederation to promote his ideas. Metternich persuaded the others to introduce the 'Karlsbad Decrees' to ensure tighter censorship. Liberal newspapers were banned, some university professors dismissed and radical leaders imprisoned. Metternich was desperate to prevent the spread of revolutionary ideas. Despite his efforts, the July 1830 revolution in Paris sparked riots in several German states. In Brunswick, the Duke was driven out and replaced, but elsewhere these uprisings came to nothing.

In 1832 Metternich persuaded the Confederation to pass the 'Six Acts', which banned public meetings, tightened control of universities and the press, and obliged German princes to resist any attempt

to reduce their power. A commission was set up to arrest student agitators who were forming themselves into a 'Young Germany' movement and campaigning for a united liberal Germany. By 1840, however, newspapers were flourishing, many books were being written and the demand for a united Germany was growing, particularly among the middle classes. Some people wanted a Germany ruled by a monarch, others wanted a republic. Some were more concerned with making life better and expanding suffrage and others were more focused on nationalism. The idea of nationalism was growing in popularity, particularly since it seemed in 1840 that France was likely to invade along the Rhine. The Press backed nationalist ideas and lots of songs and poems brought the idea to the masses.

In 1840 Frederick William IV became the new King of Prussia. For a time he seemed to want to please his people and started releasing political prisoners and abolishing censorship. After just three years, however, he had re-imposed press censorship and taken power away from local governments.

After 1815, all German states managed their own economies. Customs barriers and tariffs made trade difficult and expensive. In 1819, Prussia made agreements with neighbouring states to remove these barriers. This meant a wider market for home-produced goods at lower prices. Other German states, impressed by Prussia's success, either joined the 'Prussian Customs Union' or formed opposing unions. By 1834 the Prussian Customs Union — later known as the 'German Customs Union' or 'Zollverein' — was the most successful, incorporating eighteen states. By 1844, only Hanover, Oldenburg, Mecklenburg, the Hanseatic towns and Austria had not joined. Within the Union, all internal customs barriers were dismantled, and a start was made at unifying the currency and system of weights used. The Zollverein put Prussia in a position of leadership among German states, strengthened their economic links, and contributed to the formation of a national market. Suddenly, the idea of a politically united Germany seemed possible.

Otto von Bismarck was elected to the Prussian assembly in 1847 and was determined to make Prussia more powerful. He wanted to see a united German confederation, led by one king and protected by one army, but he wanted the King of Prussia to be that man. Unfortunately, Frederick William IV was not the strong decisive leader that Bismarck needed.

Like the rest of Europe, the German states were going through hard times in the lead up to 1848. Over 70% of Germans were land workers, and industrialisation was affecting their jobs. Some turned to machine breaking. A rapidly growing population was also causing increased poverty. The corn and potato harvests had failed making the situation even more desperate. The middle classes wanted to see changes made but were frustrated by the power of the nobility.

In 1848, following the February Revolution in France, rebellion spread to many small south-west German states. In some places peasants attacked their landlords, stormed castles and destroyed feudal records, but in most areas meetings, demonstrations and petitions were used rather than violence. Most were not interested in a full revolution; they wanted simply to change the system rather than get rid of the princes altogether. This relatively peaceful revolt attracted little support and was quickly suppressed. In most states some sort of agreement was reached and the old rulers stayed in power.

At a meeting in Heidelberg in March, fifty-one representatives from six states discussed changes to Germany's political structure and the possibility of unity. On March 5th they decided that representatives from all German peoples should meet, and invitations were quickly issued.

Meanwhile, in Prussia, a demonstration by workers took place on March 13th and troops had to be sent to preserve order. On the 18th, under pressure, Frederick William finally agreed to accept the idea of a new German constitution and a large crowd gathered outside the Royal palace to cheer the King. Attempts to clear the crowd, however, led to shots being fired. Angry students and workers immediately set up barricades and fighting erupted. Around three hundred rioters were killed as the King's troops took back control of the city. To appease the rebels, Frederick William made a personal appeal for peace. Copies of his letter 'To my dear Berliners' were distributed, promising that the troops would be withdrawn if the street barricades were taken down.

The troops were withdrawn and the King left unguarded, but the barricades were not removed. Berlin citizens formed a civic guard to protect the palace. On the 19th the King appeared on the balcony to salute the bodies of the dead rioters. On the 21st he appeared in the streets with the German colours — black, red and gold — round his arm to show his support for the demands of the people. He was greeted with huge applause when he declared that he wanted a united Germany. Bismarck was horrified to see the King bow to the will of the people and came in disguise to Berlin to offer his help. The King rejected it, but told him to regroup the army in case it was needed.

On the 31st, back in Frankfurt, five hundred and seventy-four representatives — from almost all the states in the Confederation — answered their invitations and met to discuss change. This was known as the 'Vorparlament'. After five days of debate, an agreement was reached on how to convene a national parliament. One representative for every fifty thousand inhabitants would be elected by citizens who were male, of age and 'economically independent'. Women, servants, farm labourers and anyone receiving poor relief were not included. Elections were carried out quickly and the first national parliament met in May. Nearly all its members were from the educated middle classes.

They wanted the new government to be strong and decided on the creation of a new national constitution that would overrule state laws. Deciding what the constitution should actually contain proved more difficult and no agreement was reached. They were split between a majority who wanted a monarchy and a minority that wanted a republic. They also had difficulty working out where the boundaries of a new Germany might lie. Some wanted Austria included, others did not. There were further problems with the lands of Holstein and Schleswig in the north which were ruled by Denmark. Holstein was part of the Confederation but Schleswig was not. Denmark did not want either state in a new Germany whereas the Frankfurt Assembly wished both to be included. The Danish decided to make their view clear by starting a blockade of German Harbours. The Confederation retaliated by founding a German navy and ordering Prussian troops to enter Schleswig-Holstein. The Danish demanded that these troops be removed. Under pressure from other European countries, Prussia and Denmark agreed to share administration of the area.

The Frankfurt Assembly was annoyed by this decision, especially as they had not been consulted, but were left with little option but to eventually accept it. The people were unhappy at this failure of their assembly and in September there was an uprising against it. Two members of the parliament were murdered and the assembly had to call on Austria and Prussia to help calm things down. Frederick William appointed his uncle, Count Brandenburg, as the new Prussian Prime Minister and sent him to deal with the uprising. These events undermined the position of the National Assembly. To the German revolutionaries it seemed as though their parliament was more interested in keeping the princes happy than in following the wishes of the people.

In Prussia, earlier in the year, Frederick William, had appeared to agree with his people and the idea of becoming the head of a constitutional government. Now back with his loyal army, he expressed very different views to those he had expressed on the streets of Berlin. He complained that he had been forced to make concessions and made it clear that he did not, in fact, wish to be a citizen king, answerable to the people. Count Brandenburg set about exiling revolutionaries from Berlin. The civil guard was dissolved and thousands of troops moved into Berlin. There was virtually no resistance, and the army made short work of any unrest.

In December, the Frankfurt parliament, trying to re-establish itself, approved the 'fifty articles of the fundamental rights of the German citizen'. These included equality before the law, freedom of worship, freedom of the press and an end to discrimination with regard to class. In Prussia, Frederick William decided to put forward a constitution of his own. In his parliament, ministers would be appointed and dismissed by the King, who retained total control of the army and could alter the constitution any time it suited him. While the Frankfurt Assembly opposed Frederick William's idea, the Prussians approved, and Otto von Bismarck was put in charge of their parliament.

The Frankfurt parliament, still hoping to unite Germany, needed a leader that would serve the people of Germany. Unfortunately, their options were now limited since any leader they chose would have Prussia as his enemy. They could see only one solution. They decided to try for a constitutional monarchy and, in the spring of 1849, offered Frederick William the German crown. He refused it, declaring that he was not prepared to be German emperor if it meant putting himself and Prussia under their control.

The refusal of Frederick William to accept the crown finished the Frankfurt parliament. Many of its members gave up and went home. The remnants — about a hundred and thirty of them — made a last attempt to recover the situation, calling for the election of a leader instead. It did not work. They were driven out of Frankfurt by the city government and moved to Stuttgart, the capital of the kingdom of Wurttemberg. There they were forcibly dispersed by the King's soldiers in June 1849. There were a few small uprisings but these were dealt with by Prussian troops.

The 1848 revolution had failed. Little had changed in the German states.

Revision

Were the revolutions of 1848 important?

Why were there so many revolutions in 1848?

— revolution in France made people believe that there could be change

— revolts sparked new revolts

— the people were discontented with their situation and felt that their lack of suffrage meant their views were not being heard

— the poor harvest meant people faced starvation

— industrial changes had caused unemployment

— better means of communication meant that revolutionary ideas were spread faster and more easily

— there was anger at the harsh way rebellions were dealt with, making people even more determined to force change

— there was frustration at the lack of free speech and censorship of the press

— universities were teaching students about different systems of government.

Did the revolutions have anything in common?

— a desire for liberalism

— a desire for nationalism

— a desire for improved conditions

— the demand for universal suffrage

— frustration among the people

— a desire for unity within France, Italy and Germany.

Did the revolutions change anything?

— an increase in suffrage

— a change of leadership in France

— some independence

— Prussia became dominant among the German states

— the Austrian Empire's oppression of its people grew more severe.

Why did most of the revolutions fail?

— revolutionaries lacked resources

— strong leaders wanted power for themselves rather than follow the wishes of the people

— the women and poor still had no right to vote

— there was a lack of agreement about who should rule

— in the German states, meetings and demonstrations did not convey a strong enough message, and the people still wanted the princes to rule

— in the Austrian Empire, no middle class existed to support a revolution

— in Italy, the Pope's influence led to Catholics following his lead

— other European countries became involved.

Some questions for you to try

1   Describe the overthrow of Louis Philippe in February 1848.

2   Why were there mixed reactions in France to the February revolution of 1848?

3   To what extent were other revolutions in Europe in 1848 the result of revolution in France?

4   What were the 'March Laws' of 1848 in Hungary?

5   Why did revolution fail in the Austrian Empire?

6   Why was there revolution in Italy in 1848?

7   Why was Charles Albert unsuccessful against Austria in 1848-9?

8   Describe the creation and collapse of the Roman Republic (1848-9).

9   Why did the Frankfurt Assembly fail?

10 Did revolution in Europe achieve anything?

Chapter 4

Unification within Europe

4.1 The creation of modern Italy

The 1848 revolution in the Italian states had been a failure, but the idea of creating a united Italy had not been forgotten.

In Piedmont-Sardinia, the old king, Charles Albert, had abdicated, leaving his son Victor Emanuel II on the throne. In 1852, Camillo de Cavour became the first Prime Minister of Piedmont-Sardinia. Cavour was a strong believer in the unification of Italy but, unlike the revolutionary Mazzini, who wanted a republic, he wished to see a monarchy, with the King of Piedmont-Sardinia as the King of Italy.

In order for this to happen, Cavour knew that he needed to make Piedmont-Sardinia the strongest Italian state, and focused on building up its independent economy and industry. Piedmont began taking international trade away from Austria. Cavour put money into building better railways and tried to raise living standards. He also encouraged people to become involved in government, and used the press to spread propaganda and gain a consensus. Some of his methods were a little controversial. It was suggested that he used bribery and threats to get his way, but soon people throughout Piedmont-Sardinia wanted a united Italy led by Victor Emanuel II.

Camillo de Cavour

Alliances and Tensions

The Crimean War broke out in 1853, with Britain, France and the Ottoman Turks fighting Russia. Piedmont was asked to join the alliance against Russia, mainly so that Austria would join too. Austria did not trust Piedmont-Sardinia enough to send their troops off to fight unless the latter's troops were also occupied. Piedmont-Sardinia entered the war quite near its end, but it showed the French and British their willingness to form such an alliance.

Feeling that there was a renewed desire for unification, Garibaldi returned to Italy.

The revolution in 1848 had been crushed when France became involved. Cavour knew that this time he would need France to be on his side and met Napoleon III secretly, at a French Spa in Plombieres, with a proposal. Piedmont would cause trouble in Modena, forcing Austria, which controlled the territory, to declare war on them. France would then side with Piedmont in exchange for Nice and Savoy. Napoleon III agreed. A marriage was arranged between the daughter of Victor Emanuel and the Emperor's cousin, to complete the deal.

In April 1859 Piedmont prepared for war. Before any further steps could be taken, Austria demanded they disarm. This was perfect for Piedmont as it made it look as though Austria was the aggressor. Piedmont refused and war was declared. Napoleon III kept his side of the deal and France joined Piedmont, although it took a while for their troops to mobilise. Piedmont was left on its own until the French arrived but, luckily for them, bad weather and the disorganisation of the Austrians meant that this occurred before any major fighting started. The combined forces of France and Piedmont-Sardinia won the first battles against Austria, at Magenta and Solferino. The German state of Prussia soon joined Austria, and other Italian nations joined Piedmont.

It was all going to plan, until Napoleon III started to panic. He had not foreseen Prussia's involvement and began to worry about making such a strong state an enemy. Also, more Italian states than he had expected were joining in. Their unity would ultimately make the Italians much stronger than he would like. Suddenly, he signed a treaty with Austria in July 1859. Fearing they would not be able to defeat Austria without France, Victor Emanuel II also withdrew. Cavour was furious and resigned. There were some positive results: Piedmont gained the land of Lombardy from the Austrians, and, as Napoleon III had not kept his word, it kept Nice and Savoy.

Most importantly, the war had proved that Italians were ready to unite.

Cavour only retired from politics for a short time, and by January 1860 he was back as Prime Minister and negotiating with the French. This time, Cavour offered Savoy and Nice in return for allowing Piedmont-Sardinia to annex the Italian states of Tuscany and Emilia. Once again, Napoleon III agreed, and the take-over went ahead. Many people within these two states had been keen to join with Piedmont. It was the first real step towards Italian unification.

Garibaldi's Thousand head for Sicily

Garibaldi was very angry and upset that his birthplace of Nice now belonged to the French and blamed Cavour personally for this. There was fear for a while that he might attempt to retake the city. Cavour tried to convince him that it was a small loss, set against the possibility of unification, even if the result was a monarchy rather than the republic Garibaldi desired. A resolution of the dispute was never reached as an uprising in Sicily distracted their attention.

Garibaldi gathered together an army of approximately one thousand volunteers and headed for Sicily to help the rebels. Cavour neither aided nor opposed him, although Victor Emanuel II favoured assistance. Garibaldi landed his ships on the shores of the island, and marched his army towards Palermo — one of its most important cities. Poor farmers and peasants flooded into this army, hoping to free themselves from the rule of the Bourbon king. The King's army came to Palermo to drive out the invaders, but without success. Within two months, the unskilled, ill-equipped army, known as the Red Shirts, had taken Sicily. Garibaldi declared himself dictator, in the name of Victor Emanuel II.

Cavour was worried about the power Garibaldi had over the people, and the greater power he would gain if he successfully took the southern states. He therefore tried to persuade him to hand over Sicily to Piedmont and end the fighting. Cavour even managed to get the King to write a letter expressing these wishes, even though it is believed that Victor Emanuel still supported Garibaldi.

The letter did not stop Garibaldi, or his army.

Garibaldi heads for Naples

Garibaldi sailed his army, which had grown to around twenty-five thousand, to the shores of Naples, with the help of the British Navy. It was at this time that Mazzini, who had returned to Italy in 1856, joined him. Less than three months after their arrival in the south of Italy, they met the soldiers of the Neapolitan army in battle at the Volturno River, in the centre of Naples. Garibaldi was victorious, and now ruled the whole southern part of Italy. Finding himself in a powerful position, he demanded publicly that Cavour be removed from power. Although Cavour kept his job, Garibaldi's statement began to drive a wedge between Victor Emanuel and his Prime Minister.

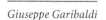

Giuseppe Garibaldi

After the conquest of Naples, the war should have ended, but Garibaldi announced they would not stop there, as originally planned, but that they would also take Rome, linking his states with those ruled by Piedmont.

Tensions between Garibaldi and Cavour

Cavour became even more worried by this. If Rome was attacked, France and Austria would both fight together again to protect the Pope. Cavour had another idea: if Garibaldi could be encouraged to take the Papal states, rather than Rome itself, then the territories might be joined without upsetting Catholics. Cavour sent the Piedmontese army out to take the northern Papal States and prevent Garibaldi from attacking Rome. When Garibaldi's army arrived, two thirds of the Papal States had joined Piedmont and the rest rushed to join him. There was no longer any need to attack Rome.

Thanks to Cavour, a much larger war had been avoided.

On September 18th 1860, Victor Emanuel and Garibaldi met. There is a great deal of controversy about what happened at this meeting and even the location was kept secret, but by the end of the day Garibaldi had handed over control of his army and the land he had taken to Victor Emanuel.

Italy was finally unified in 1861, with Victor Emanuel its first king. It was not a republic as Garibaldi and Mazzini had hoped, but it *was* a single state.

Despite unification, it was not yet the Italy of today. Rome was still independent, and Venetia was still ruled by the Austrians. An opportunity to change this came in 1866, when Austria and Prussia went to war with each other. Austria promised to give Venetia to Italy if they did not get involved, and Prussia promised to win it for Italy if it joined their side. Italy chose Prussia. Although the Italian army was not very useful, Prussia won and kept its promise. Venetia became part of Italy.

In 1870, France and Prussia went to war. While France was preoccupied, Italy saw a perfect opportunity to at last unite with Rome. Italian troops marched into the city unopposed and Rome joined the union. In July 1871, it became the capital of the new, fully unified, Italy.

In the years that followed unification, Mazzini continued unsuccessfully to campaign for a republic. He refused a place in the new government, but continued to voice his opinions until his death in 1872. However, Italy was unified, and Cavour, Garibaldi and Mazzini would go down in history as the founding fathers of a new nation.

King Victor Emanuel of Italy

Revision

How was Italy unified?

Why was Italy not unified in 1848-1850?

— the Pope had called for help and refused to take sides

— people could not agree on how they wanted to be ruled: by president, Pope or king

— the Austrians held too much power in Italy and the revolt against them had failed

— each state wanted something different

— the involvement of France proved to be too great a threat.

How important was Garibaldi's contribution to unifying Italy?

— he was one of Mazzini's men and wanted a republic

— he returned to Italy when feelings of unification were at a high

— Cavour's political moves provided him with opportunity

— he invaded Sicily and Naples (with Mazzini's help)

— he handed power to the King in 1861.

How important for other European countries were moves towards Italian unification?

— France was threatened by Italian unification

— it meant loss of territory and power for Austria

— Catholics did not want to see the Pope threatened.

Did Cavour help or hinder the unification of Italy?

— he was Prime Minister of Piedmont-Sardinia

— he wanted unification with a king in charge

— he focused on making Piedmont-Sardinia the strongest state

— he persuaded Napoleon III to side with him in a war against Austria; France panicked and pulled out, but the war had showed that the Italian people were ready for unity

— he gave Italian land to France, upsetting Garibaldi

63

— he did not want Garibaldi gaining too much power

— he prevented Garibaldi from attacking Rome.

Some questions for you to try

1   Why did revolutions in Italy in 1848–49 fail?

2   What role did Mazzini play in the unification of Italy?

3   Did Garibaldi or Cavour play the more important rôle?

4   Could Italy have been unified without Garibaldi?

5   How important a part did Napoleon III play?

4.2 The creation of modern Germany

King Frederick William of Prussia had refused to accept the imperial crown offered by the Frankfurt Parliament, but he was still attracted to the idea of a united Germany with himself at its head, providing he had the consent of the princes.

The Erfurt Union

In 1849 Prussian statesman Joseph Radowitz came up with the 'Prussian Union' plan. He proposed a 'Kleindeutschreich' — a 'Little German Kingdom' — excluding Austria, and under Prussian leadership. In addition, there would be a 'German Union', a confederation similar to the old one, which would include both the new Reich and the Austrian Empire. This did not find favour with the Austrian Chief Minister, Prince Felix of Schwarzenberg, who saw it just as a way of removing Austrian influence from Germany. However, as Schwarzenberg was busy dealing with a Hungarian uprising, Prussia was able to continue with its plan.

In March 1850, representatives from most of the German states met at Erfurt in Prussia. Twenty-eight states agreed to the creation of the Prussian dominated 'Erfurt Union', but several were suspicious of Prussia, and too fearful of Austria to agree.

The Frankfurt Diet

Austrian minister Schwarzenberg, having suppressed the Hungarian revolt, was ready to reassert Austria's position in Germany. He summoned a Diet of the Confederation, to meet in Frankfurt in May 1850. The response was good. Now there were two assemblies, both wanting to speak for Germany, the Prussian-led Erfurt Parliament and the Austrian-led Frankfurt Diet.

The Treaty of Olmutz

The power of these two assemblies was soon to be tested when an uprising occurred in the state of Hesse-Cassel. Although a member of the Erfurt Union, its ruler requested help from the Frankfurt Diet, which sent Bavarian troops to restore order. The Erfurt Union dispatched Prussian troops. It looked as though conflict would begin between the two opposing armies, but Prussia backed down, worried that Russia might join in on Austria's side.

Humiliated by these events, Frederick William agreed to abolish the Erfurt Union, as part of the Treaty of Olmutz. This was a big victory for Austria and the Habsburgs. Schwarzenberg quickly proposed a new union — an Austria-dominated 'Middle Europe', incorporating the seventy million people of the German states along with the Habsburg empire. This proposal was rejected, and in May 1851 the state representatives decided to restore the old confederation instead.

Nothing had changed. Austria remained powerful.

The strengthening of Prussia

Prussian Chief Minister Otto von Manteuffel, decided to concentrate on Prussian affairs. He wanted to strengthen the country and reduce the chance of revolution, by improving living conditions for the peasants and workers. He imposed press censorship and restricted the freedom of political parties to hold meetings. Industrial production, railway building and foreign trade all doubled. It was a good year for agriculture also, and living standards rose.

Manteuffel also wanted to improve Prussia's political power and looked at expanding the Zollverein (trade agreements). He proposed a trade union that included Austria, but Austria turned it down. He tried again with an alternative customs union, including not just Austria but all the states outside the Zollverein, but again it was rejected. Austria was not prepared to give up any of its power.

Instead, he turned his attention towards Prussia's relationships with its other neighbours. When the Crimean War began, Prussia opted to stay on good terms with the Russians, whereas Austria chose to join the fight against them.

In 1859, when Piedmont and France went to war with Austria over Italian lands, Prussia had again to decide which side to take. On this occasion it chose Austria, as Prussians were in general more anti-French than anti-Austrian. Had they chosen to take France's side, the war might have reduced Austria's power in Germany, but they chose to side with Austria, in return for a promise to allow Prussia to become the dominant German state. As Austria then lost the war, this came to nothing.

The Army Reform Bill

During this spate of conflict, the leadership in Prussia also changed. In 1858, after a series of strokes had left him blind and unable to speak, Frederick William was declared insane. His brother Wilhelm became regent until the King's death in 1861, when he became Wilhelm I, at the age of sixty-three. Wilhelm had been a soldier and set about strengthening Prussia's army. With the help of Albrecht von Roon and Helmuth von Molkte, a bill was proposed to reform the army, with the aims of doubling its size, increasing the period of service from two to three years, reducing the role of the civilian militia and re-equipping the troops. Although this would strengthen Prussia's power, some were worried about the cost, and others about whether a more powerful army might be used to oppress its own people.

Wilhelm wanted to take full control of the army but parliament had financial control. In 1860, Parliament would only agree to approve the increased military budget for one year, and not to extend the term of military service. Annoyed, Wilhelm dismissed Manteuffel and had a new parliament elected in December 1861. But this one would neither extend military service *nor* increase the military budget. Wilhelm once again dissolved Parliament, and replaced all the ministers who disagreed with him. However, the following May, when elections came round, it was the men he had removed who were voted back in. Once again, the army bill was turned down.

Fearing civil war, Wilhelm considered abdicating but instead, under advice, he made Otto von Bismarck, a leading politician during his brother's reign, chief minister. Bismarck was confident he could sort out the crisis. Initially, his main aim was for Prussia to dominate the northern states, rather than the whole country. He was more interested in making Prussia powerful than creating a united Germany, but he was not opposed to unification, as long as Prussia was in charge. He was also aware that unification was a popular concept amongst the German people.

Bismarck solved the problem of the military budget by withdrawing the bill and declaring that the support of Parliament was unnecessary as the army could be financed from taxes. The taxes were collected and the army reorganised, with Parliament having no say. For the next four years, Bismarck commanded the army, and twice went to war, without including Parliament in any decision. New elections in 1863 gave parliamentary seats to even more members who disagreed with him, but Bismarck continued with his plans, believing that he would eventually prove that his methods were best.

Relations and Tensions

In 1863 revolts broke out in the Polish areas of Russia. Disliking Poles, and considering them trouble makers, Bismarck offered his support. Russia declined, but an agreement was reached that allowed Russian soldiers to cross into Prussia when in pursuit of Polish rebels.

This friendship with Russia worried France and Britain.

The Danish king, Frederick VII, died in 1863 without an heir, and the throne passed to a distant relative, Christian IX. This caused immediate problems in the Danish-controlled German states of Schleswig and Holstein who, following Salic Law, had a slightly different rule regarding succession. The leading families in Schleswig and Holstein, who felt they had more right to the throne of these two states, put forward their own claimant, the German Duke of Augustenburg.

Christian IX escalated the tension by announcing that Schleswig was now part of Denmark. The German Confederation was furious and sent an army on behalf of the Duke. This gave Bismarck a wonderful opportunity. He could see a way to take control of the two states, strengthen Prussian power and win credit for himself. Bismarck claimed that he supported the Duke and persuaded Austria to help him. Independently, both Austria and Prussia sent troops against Denmark.

Faced with such opposition and a lack of support from elsewhere in Europe, Christian IX gave up his claim on the two German states and handed them over to Austria and Prussia. Austria and the rest of the confederacy expected power to pass to the Duke, but Bismarck had other plans, only agreeing while Prussia held power over him. Austria was furious with Prussia, but war was avoided because Austria was suffering financial difficulties and Wilhelm I was reluctant to fight a fellow German state. In the end, they agreed that Austria would have Holstein and Prussia Schleswig. Bismarck was happy with this as he knew he could pick a fight with Austria over Holstein any time he wanted.

Bismarck then turned his attention to France and met with Napoleon III in October 1865. He was reluctant to give France any land in exchange for French support. Napoleon, not sure who the winning side would be in a war between Prussia and Austria, decided

Otto von Bismarck

to remain neutral. He felt that mediation between the two would put France in the strongest position, and assured Bismarck it would stay out of the fight.

Over the winter of 1865, Prussian/Austrian relations grew worse. While Prussia had the support of several small north-German states, the largest ones sided with Austria. By February 1866, war was inevitable and imminent. However, it would no longer be a war to settle the fate of Schleswig and Holstein, but to decide who would control the whole of Germany. In April, Bismarck arranged an alliance with Italy, stating that if war started within three months, and Italy sided with Prussia, they would receive Venetia in return, as long as Prussia won. Austria started to mobilise her forces, in preparation for a surprise attack. Claiming that it was responding to Austria's obvious aggression, Prussia began mobilising its troops as well.

Austria appealed to the Confederation, on June 1st 1866, to settle the future of Schleswig and Holstein. According to Bismarck, this broke their agreement, and he promptly sent his troops to occupy Holstein. Austria was permitted to withdraw its troops peacefully from the area. To Bismarck's amazement this did *not* immediately lead to war.

On June 10th, he proposed that the Confederation be reorganised to exclude Austria, that a national parliament be elected by national suffrage and that all troops in northern Germany be placed under Prussian control. The next day, Austria asked the Diet to reject Bismarck's plan and prepare for war. It was indeed rejected. Prussia withdrew from the Confederation, declared it dissolved and invited all German states to ally themselves with her against Austria. Instead, most began mobilising their troops to fight *Prussia*. Bismarck issued an ultimatum to Hanover, Hesse-Cassel and Saxony: join Prussia or become its enemy. They refused, so he invaded all three, forcing them into an alliance.

Austria and Prussia at war

War with Austria was imminent and the future of Bismarck, Prussia and Germany all lay in the hands of General Moltke and the Prussian army, but they were strong. Prussian military expenditure had doubled since 1860, while that of Austria had halved. They also had much better equipment, including guns that fired five times faster than those of the Austrians. On the other hand, Austria had more soldiers, more support from the other German states and a more central location. However, it also faced a threat of revolt by the Italian states it ruled, so it could not give war with Prussia its full attention.

Prussia advanced its troops into Bohemia. Only one railway line led from Austria to Bohemia, whereas five ran from Prussia. This meant that Prussia could move its troops faster, but ran a risk in dividing them. Austria missed the opportunity this presented and the two armies met at Koniggratz in July. Here, the Prussians had the much stronger position. Seeing that her situation was hopeless, Austria quickly asked for a peace treaty, to protect her empire. Wilhelm wanted to continue the war, but Bismarck, fearful that France and Russia might intervene, insisted they sign the treaty. In a heated meeting on July 23rd, Bismarck got his way by threatening suicide, and a peace was created.

Prussia gained Holstein and gave Italy the land it had promised.

With Austria defeated, Bismarck could have now pushed for unification, but he feared the threat of foreign intervention and that forcing states to unite would cause more trouble. Instead he proposed a military alliance where all states would put their armies under the control of the Prussian king, in the event of war. Amazingly, the states agreed. It seems they were too afraid of Bismarck to disagree, and felt they would be safer in an alliance, especially should France attack.

The Franco-Prussian War

In 1867 the Dutch King agreed to sell Luxembourg to France, subject to the approval of the King of Prussia. Bismarck decided to hand the decision over to the other European leaders. At a conference in London, it was decided that Luxemburg should become neutral. Napoleon III was very upset at this outcome and relations between France and Prussia were damaged.

The following year was fairly peaceful. Bismarck was keen to avoid war as he feared French military strength and the possibility Napoleon would find allies — especially since the Austrian Emperor, Francis Joseph, had met twice with Napoleon regarding an Austrian takeover of Germany.

In 1868, following a revolution in Spain, the Spanish government requested that Prince Leopold, a relation of Wilhelm I, become their new king. Bismarck thought this a good idea, as Prussia would then have Spain as an ally. Wilhelm was less keen because he knew Napoleon would feel encircled and see this as a threat. Despite his doubts, Wilhelm was encouraged to support the idea. Leopold, however, turned the offer down as he did not want to make an enemy of France. It looked as though, once again, trouble had been averted, but Bismarck was not prepared to let the matter drop. He persuaded Leopold to reconsider. Under pressure, Leopold agreed and Wilhelm gave his formal consent.

When news of what had happened arrived in Paris there was uproar. Napoleon III threatened war if Leopold took the title. Wilhelm panicked and declared that Leopold would withdraw his acceptance. Bismarck was humiliated and threatened resignation. Napoleon then took things one step further and demanded that Wilhelm publicly renounce all support for Leopold. Wilhelm was

King Wilhelm I of Prussia

annoyed that his word was not enough and at being pressured by France, but he duly sent a telegram to Bismarck instructing him to release the statement to the press. On receiving the telegram, Bismarck altered some words before passing it to the press, making it sound instead like a snub to France. The French were furious. Convinced their honour was at stake, newspapers and crowds demanded war, which was declared on July 19th 1870. With its declaration of war, Bismarck claimed that France was the aggressor and called upon the southern states for support, in accordance with the terms of their military alliance with Prussia. Convinced that the fatherland was in danger, they agreed.

The German troops mobilised quickly — much faster than the French. The Prussians had six railway lines to the French frontier, the French had only two. When the armies met, things did not go well for the French. Napoleon III was captured and the French had to sign an armistice. As a result, France had to give up Alsace-Lorraine, which led to long-lasting animosity between it and Germany.

German unification

The war created a wave of German patriotism, and a feeling among the public that a permanent union of German states would be best. After persuasion and a little bribery, treaties were signed in November 1870. The new 'Second Reich' was a federation. Each member state retained their monarchy and power over internal affairs, but overall political power was placed in the hands of an emperor.

The German Empire was proclaimed on 18th January 1871, with Wilhelm as Emperor and Bismarck Imperial Chancellor.

At last Prussia was the strongest state in a German kingdom, just as Bismarck had dreamed.

Revision

How was Germany Unified?

Why was Germany not unified in 1848-1850?

- — the German people still wanted their princes

- — they held meetings and demonstrations rather than use violence

- — Austria refused to join

- — Frederick William refused the title from the Frankfurt Parliament

- — there was a lack of agreement on the way a united Germany should be ruled.

How did Bismarck bring about Austria's defeat of 1866?

— he wanted unification, as long as Prussia was in charge

— he took control of the army

— he built good relations with Russia

— he tricked Austria into helping him gain Danish lands, which left bad feelings that could erupt at any time

— Austria was preoccupied with revolt in the Italian states

— he ensured the army was well financed and better equipped

— better Prussian railways meant quicker mobilisation giving the army an advantage, even though Austria's army was bigger.

How did Bismarck bring about France's defeat of 1870?

— he upset Napoleon III over the sale of Luxemburg, asking other European countries to decide, with the result that the sale was refused

— Wilhelm's cousin Leopold was persuaded to take the throne of Spain, therefore surrounding France, but Leopold was too worried by France's reaction to take the title

— he altered the letter from Wilhelm and published it in the press in order to start a confrontation with France

— the Prussian army was prepared and mobilised quickly

— better railways gave Prussia an advantage in speed of deployment.

How far was Bismarck responsible for the unification of Germany?

— he put Prussia in a dominant position

— he built up relations with neighbouring countries

— he ensured Prussia was in a stronger position than Austria

— he manipulated situations and repeatedly portrayed the other country as the aggressor

— with France declaring war, other states moved to support Prussia

— he helped create a feeling of unity by forcing the separate states into a position where they had to stand together.

Some questions for you to try

1 What was the Zollverein?

2 In what ways were the Prussian armed forces reformed?

3 Why was the Frankfurt Parliament created?

4 What was the Treaty of Olmutz?

5 Why did the Schleswig-Holstein issue cause problems?

6 Why did France declare war on Prussia in 1870?

7 What effect did the Franco-Prussian war have?

8 Could unification have occurred without Bismarck?

Chapter 5

Civil War in the United States

5.1 Slavery

The idea of slavery is a very old one that has existed throughout history. During the 16th century many African slaves were transported from Africa to the Americas, along one side of the 'Triangular Trade Route'. The first Africans arrived in North America during the early days of British colonisation, in 1619. Slavery developed quite slowly there until the tobacco trade created a demand for more workers. By the middle of the 18th century there were hundreds of thousands of slaves working the land. The demand for slaves decreased as tobacco production declined, only to increase again with the introduction of cotton as a plantation crop, particularly after the invention of Eli Whitney's cotton 'gin' (engine) in 1793. This separated the fibre from the seed — a job previously completed by hand. It made quicker preparation of cotton possible, and therefore required the raw material to be harvested more rapidly.

Vast quantities of cotton were shipped to Great Britain to supply the expanding textile industry.

Many slaves were transported to North America from Africa at this time, and sold at auction. Higher prices were paid for healthy, young slaves who had been trained by previous owners, or those that possessed valuable skills. They were often given European names in an attempt to make them forget their African past. Some owners had them branded like cattle with their owner's initials or mark on their face, chest or shoulder. Not all slaves worked on plantations: skilled slaves were often bought by companies to work in places such as saw mills, mines and fisheries. They were also used to build roads, canals, bridges and railways.

Freedom

Occasionally slaves managed to buy their freedom. If their masters allowed it, they could hire them-selves to others for a fee. Half of the money had to be given to their owners, but the other half could be saved towards the price of their freedom — an amount set by their owner. The purchase of liberty was called 'manumission' and freed slaves were known as 'free blacks'.

Other slaves chose running away as a means to find freedom and many headed towards Canada via the 'Underground Railway'. This did not refer to a real railway, but to a route used by escaped slaves and the people along the way willing to help. Tens of thousands escaped this way, travelling north using the North Star. The hiding places along the route were called 'stations', and those who helped them 'conductors'. So many slaves escaped that a law was passed in 1793, making it illegal to hide runaways.

End of the slave trade

In the late 18th and early 19th century, many people in America and Europe began to call for an end to slavery. They were called 'abolitionists'. The earliest abolition society was founded in Britain in 1787. Its founder, Thomas Clarkson, travelled throughout Britain speaking out against the slave trade, and per-suading people not to buy slave-grown produce. He enlisted the help of politician William Wilberforce, who spoke out in Parliament and spent the next twenty years campaigning for abolition.

The British Government finally ended the slave trade in 1807. No more slaves would be carried from Africa in British ships. The United States of America (USA) followed suit, but this did not stop them breeding more slaves at home.

Rebellion

Throughout the history of the enslavement of Africans, there is evidence of slaves resisting and fighting back. The bloodiest revolt in the USA occurred on August 21st 1831 when Nat Turner and six other slaves in Southampton County, Virginia, attacked their owners in their beds. Turner had apparently seen visions and heard voices which told him to rebel against the white masters. During the next few days, over fifty white slave owners were murdered as others joined the rebellion. Turner and many of his followers were eventually captured and hanged.

On October 16th 1859, a white abolitionist called John Brown attempted to start a slave rebellion in the town of Harper's Ferry in Virginia. He planned to break into the local arsenal and give captured weapons to the town slaves so that they could join his 'freedom army'. With just twenty-one followers, including his own sons and some ex-slaves, Brown captured the arsenal. He took several hostages as well as weapons, including Colonel Lewis Washington, a local slave owner and great-great nephew of the first president, George Washington. Several shots were fired including one which killed railway baggage porter and freed slave, Hayward Shepherd. Brown did not get very far. The militia and other townsfolk quickly gathered their own weapons and trapped Brown and his men in the engine house adjacent to the arsenal. The engine house was finally stormed by US Marines, led by one Lieutenant Colonel Robert E. Lee. Nine of Brown's followers were killed, including two of his sons. One free black managed to escape, and was never captured. The remaining rebels, including John Brown, were publicly hanged in Charlestown, Virginia, later that year.

Although many northerners disapproved of John Brown's methods, his attempted rebellion persuaded others that slavery in the USA had to be abolished. However, it also convinced many southerners that slavery had to be *defended*.

The great majority of slaves did not take part in any spectacular revolt but showed their defiance and contempt for slave owning whites in their daily lives. Slave owners often remarked on the solidarity of slaves and the fact that it was very unusual for one to betray another. This strong sense of community probably helped them deal with the appalling treatment they received.

Abolition

From the mid-1770s, individual northern states began to abolish slavery. In 1820, after America bought Louisiana from the French, the 'Missouri Compromise' banned slavery in this area, north of the parallel 36° 30′. By 1827, slavery was banned throughout the North.

The first abolitionists wanted slave owners to be given compensation, but as time went on they began to take a tougher attitude. In 1829, a man called David Walker published a pamphlet calling on slaves to use force where necessary to ensure freedom.

Between 1830 and 1840, the abolition movement grew in strength. William Garrison, a white man, set up an abolitionist newspaper called the *Liberator* in 1833. The American Anti-Slavery Society was established at the same time. Within five years, its membership had grown to a quarter of a million, including both white and black people. Many ex-slaves became active abolitionists. Some spoke out in public or, when literate, wrote memoirs of their lives in slavery, as part of the campaign.

Frederick Douglass was born a slave in Maryland in 1818 but escaped in 1838. He wrote a best-selling autobiography about his time in slavery which highlighted their plight. He was a brilliant public speaker, and travelled all over the world raising support for the abolitionist movement.

Harriet Tubman was born a slave in Maryland in 1821. After twenty-five years of slavery, she escaped from her master but continued to return south to rescue others. She made numerous trips leading slaves to freedom along the 'Underground Railway'.

Sojourner Truth escaped slavery in 1827 and became a leading public speaker for the abolitionist movement. She also dictated her memoirs which were later published.

Harriet Beecher Stowe, a white abolitionist published the novel *Uncle Tom's Cabin* in 1852. This told the story of a downtrodden slave and became a best-selling book. Over three hundred thousand copies were sold in the first year, and raised a lot of support for the abolitionist cause.

5.2 Tensions between the North and South

Trade, industry, and representation

During the years 1830-1860, conflict grew between the North and the South over the issue of slavery. At this time, every state was allowed to decide for itself whether or not people could own slaves.

In the southern states, slavery was legal. Farmers made their living by growing huge fields of tobacco and cotton and needed many workers to weed, tend, and pick them. They claimed they could only afford to grow these crops if they had plenty of free labour, and therefore, without slavery, farming in the South would collapse.

In the northern states, slavery was illegal. The majority did not have huge fields full of crops that needed tending: they had factories, mills, and ironworks instead. They were going through an industrial revolution and needed workers in their factories. Some factory owners believed that, if freed, the slaves would leave the South and provide the cheap labour they needed in the North.

Slavery was not the only issue on which the North and South disagreed. The North wanted tariffs on imported foreign goods to encourage Americans to buy American products. The mainly agricultural South depended on trade, and was therefore against tariffs. Taxes were levied on exports, which made American goods more expensive for other countries to buy. Many southerners claimed that these were applied to *their* produce, but not always to Northern goods of equal value.

During these years, political power in the Federal Government, centred in Washington, D. C.,[1] was shifting. Each state elected representatives according to the number of citizens living there. In the North, the population was rapidly increasing, giving them more representatives and thus more

---

[1] 'D. C.' denotes 'District of Columbia', which is separate from any state in the union. As a result, no state can claim the power that might follow holding the capital.

influence in government. In contrast, the southern states lost political power because the population did not increase as rapidly and because slaves did not count as citizens.

Sectionalism

As the differences between the North and the South became more noticeable, people began to refer to the nation in sections. The southern states felt they were not being treated fairly and that they would be better off if they were free of federal authority in Washington. Many southerners also believed that state laws should carry more weight than federal ones, and that they should follow state regulations first. This issue was called 'states' rights'.

As the population continued to grow, more and more people started building homes and families in the new western territories. When a territory had a large enough population, it would become a state and have the opportunity to elect a representative in government. Many disputes followed regarding slavery in these territories. The Missouri Compromise of 1820 had already declared slavery illegal in the northern territories, but the southern territories had no such ruling. Many argued that slavery should be allowed in the new territories while others argued against it. The debate became very bitter.

In order to resolve this disagreement, 'The Compromise of 1850' was created. This was a series of five bills which attempted to deal with slavery in the southern territories fairly. It was decided that in California slavery would be illegal but in New Mexico and Utah the people would be allowed to use popular sovereignty to decide the issue. Slavery would also be abolished in the District of Columbia, where congress meets. Included in the Compromise was The Fugitive Slave Act, which made any federal official who did not arrest a runaway slave liable to a fine.

The Dred Scott decision

The fact that different states had different laws was very problematic at times. One particularly significant case was that of Dred Scott.

Scott was born a slave in Virginia but taken to Missouri in 1830. When his master died two years later, he was sold to an army surgeon, Dr. John Emerson. He travelled with his master, spending two and a half years in the free state of Illinois and a similar amount of time in the Wisconsin Territory. Although both areas had abolished slavery, Scott did not claim his freedom. This may have been because he was happy with his master or because he did not understand his rights. He was allowed some rights, however, and was permitted to marry Harriet Robinson.

Slaves were not usually permitted to marry as they were forbidden from entering into any legal contract. Harriet was also a slave and her ownership at this time was transferred to Emerson. When Emerson's job took him to Louisiana, a slave holding state, he left Scott and his wife in Wisconsin. A little over a year later, they travelled down the Mississippi River to meet Emerson, and continued to serve him until he died in 1843. Their ownership was then transferred to Emerson's widow, who hired them out to another army captain. At this point, Scott tried to buy his freedom, but Mrs. Emerson refused the offer.

In 1846, he was helped by abolitionists to *sue* for his freedom, claiming he should be free as he had lived in free states with his master for many years. The case was debated for many years and eventually went all the way to the United States Supreme Court. Throughout, technicalities got in the way. First, Scott had to try and prove who owned him before the case could be tried. Second, as he and his masters came from different states, no one knew whether the courts had the power to make a decision, or whether a slave had the right to take his masters to court.

In March 1857, Scott lost the case when seven out of nine Justices of the Supreme Court declared that no slave or descendant of a slave could be a US citizen. Therefore he had no rights and could not have his case tried in a Federal Court. Dred and Harriet were to remain slaves.

The ruling affected the status of every enslaved *and free* black in the United States. Now no person of African descent had any rights, even though five states had allowed free blacks to be full voting citizens since the Declaration of Independence in 1776.

The Supreme Court also ruled that Congress had no right to outlaw slavery in any of the new territories and declared the Missouri Compromise of 1820 to be 'unconstitutional'. It declared that the Compromise violated the Fifth Amendment to the Constitution which prohibits Congress from depriving persons of their property without due process of law.

Many northerners were shocked by the Court's decision, whereas many southerners approved. A politician called Abraham Lincoln was appalled by the ruling and publicly spoke out against it.

As a result of this case, the political gap between the North and the South widened.

Lincoln becomes President

Abraham Lincoln was a lawyer and Republican politician who had often spoken out against slavery, although he chose his words carefully as he knew that being too keen an abolitionist would adversely affect his career. During the 1850s, he spoke frequently of his hatred of slavery, of how it divided the country, and of how America could not be strong until everyone agreed to outlaw it.

At the end of 1860, he was elected President, due to take office in March 1861. Many southerners were Democrats, and were unhappy with this election. Lincoln had won solely on votes in the North, where there were so many more voters, and they felt the South had not been represented

Abraham Lincoln

fairly. His views on slavery could seriously damage the Southern way of life. Immediately, there was talk about southern states leaving the existing union and forming a body of their own.

Lincoln vowed he would not let this happen. He was going to keep the country united and make the new western territories free of slavery.

5.3 War and its aftermath

Secession

In December 1860, South Carolina declared their withdrawal from the United States, followed in February by Mississippi, Florida, Alabama, Georgia, Louisiana and Texas. Instead, they would form their own country — the Confederate States of America. Jefferson Davis was elected its first president.

Over the next few weeks, the Confederate States demanded that United States soldiers be removed from forts on their territory. Although some soldiers were relocated, those stationed at Fort Sumter, in South Carolina, were reinforced. The Confederates again demanded that the soldiers leave the area and turn the fort over to the new Confederate army instead. On behalf of the United States, Abraham Lincoln, now sworn in as President, refused. Confederate soldiers laid siege to the fort and within two days forced its commander and his men to surrender.

Lincoln had to decide how the United States would respond. The next morning, he published a proclamation in newspapers across the country, declaring war on the Confederate States. Many people in the North gathered together, cheering, making speeches, and singing.

Not every state was pleased that Lincoln was going to war. Two days later, Virginia joined the Confederates and, a month later, three more states — Arkansas, Tennessee, and North Carolina — left the Union for the Confederacy as well. Along the border between the North and South, the states of Kentucky, Missouri, West Virginia, Maryland, and Delaware sent a message to the President saying they would not join the Confederacy, but neither would they fight for the Union.

At first, the United States government thought that the war would be over quickly. Officials and their wives even went to watch the earliest battles of the war, as though they were a play. They were sure that the blue-coated Union soldiers would easily defeat the gray-uniformed Confederates. Lincoln soon realised this was not to

Jefferson Davis

be the case. He tried hiring Garibaldi, who had just led and won the Italian revolution, but he would not leave Italy. Instead, Ulysses S. Grant became Lincoln's general.

In the South, having also turned down Lincoln, the Virginian general Robert E. Lee led the Confederate Army. Lee did not approve of slavery, but neither was he happy with the way the southern states were represented in federal government. When Virginia left the Union, he chose to be loyal to his home state and fight for the Confederates.

War splits the country

Battles were fought all over the United States as brother fought against brother. Sometimes the Union soldiers had the advantage and sometimes the Confederates won. Thousands of men were killed.

Slaves in Virginia, learning of the northern declaration of war, began to arrive at the camps of the Union soldiers in large numbers hoping to find freedom. Unsure about what to do with such huge numbers of people, Major-General Benjamin F. Butler,

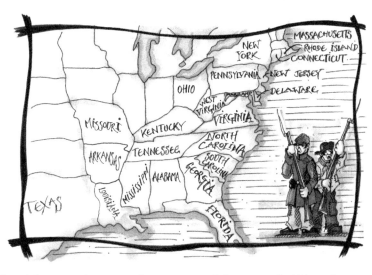

declared them to be 'contraband of war', because they were the property of the enemy.[2] Although the Northerners did not keep slaves, they still considered them a commodity. Here they were put to work digging trenches, building forts, or labouring on captured plantations. Others were sent to the North to work in mills and factories. Former slaves could be employed on much lower wages than white labourers. Many employers increased their profits by hiring them and dismissing their existing staff. Many northern workers found themselves replaced and out of a job.

The first attempt to recruit 'contraband' into the Union army as soldiers was made by Major-General David Hunter at Port Royal, South Carolina, in April 1862. Known as the 'First South Carolina Contraband Brigade' or the 'National Negro Brigade', they were poorly clothed and badly paid. Many whites refused to accept this development, so they did not officially become part of the Union Army until later, when they were renamed the 'First Carolina Volunteer Regiment' and finally provided with proper clothing and equipment. Once formally in the army, these free blacks often faced unfair treat-

---

2 'Contraband' — illegal or smuggled goods.

ment and discrimination. During the last three years of the Civil War, black regiments in the Union army took part in more than thirty major battles, impressing white soldiers with their bravery.

While many slaves had fled to the Union army, many others were being used unofficially by the Confederates as labourers to dig trenches and to build fortifications for their war effort. Many slave owners objected to this and tried to get their 'property' back. The Confederates even considered using them to fight in their army, but the idea was rejected in case it caused a slave revolt.

A year after the civil war began, Abraham Lincoln announced that all slaves in the Confederacy would be declared free on January 1st 1863. This was known as the 'Emancipation Proclamation'. Lincoln had no power in the Confederacy but his proclamation gave freedom to fleeing Southern slaves. It also declared openly that the Civil War was no longer merely about keeping the United States together: it was now being fought to end slavery as well. Lincoln needed to keep up morale and assure the people of the United States that the war was important, when hundreds of thousands of men were suffering and dying, and hundreds of towns and cities had been destroyed. He also needed to make it clear to the rest of the world just how committed he was, in order to deter any other country from joining in on the Confederates' side.

Convinced he would ultimately win, Lincoln was also busy preparing plans for reconstruction when the war finally ended. In December 1863, he announced his Reconstruction Plan, and declared that any state which had seceded would be readmitted to the Union, as soon as they accepted presidential decisions on the subject of slavery and took oaths of allegiance to the Constitution. He also announced that once one tenth of the voters who had participated in the 1860 election had taken the oath within a particular state, that state could then launch a new government and elect representatives to Congress. The states of Louisiana, Arkansas and Tennessee started to make moves to fulfil these conditions, but Lincoln's Reconstruction Plan was rejected by Congress.

The end of the war

During the American Civil War, the Union had a number of advantages over the Confederacy. The Union Army was larger, particularly after free black soldiers had joined. The North also had an established manufacturing industry, so had access to more weapons and bullets, and a better railway system, allowing supplies and troops to be moved quickly. It also possessed a navy — something the Confederates lacked. Lincoln used it to establish a blockade, preventing trade and supplies from entering or leaving the Confederate states.

The Confederate States, however, had an advantage in defending. They were not trying to conquer territory or force people to obey laws: they just wanted to defend their current way of life, and were fighting for what they believed in. The Confederates were hoping to receive support from other countries, particularly England and France, who relied on the cotton they produced. These countries failed to offer any support, especially after Lincoln's Emancipation Proclamation. Neither wanted to be seen to be supporting slavery, even though their trade and economy depended on it.

With neither support nor access to supplies, the Confederacy began to weaken. Four years after the war started, and desperate for more men, General Lee asked that slaves and free blacks be armed. On March 13th 1865, a desperate Confederate government tried to enlist three hundred thousand black men into special regiments. These soldiers would have seen minimal fighting though, as within a month the war was over.

On April 9th 1865, after being overwhelmed by Union soldiers, and realising that his Confederate army was out of food, tired and too weak to fight on, Robert E. Lee agreed to surrender.

It was now up to Lincoln to bring the states which had seceded back into the Union.

The murder of Lincoln

On April 14th, after spending the day meeting with his advisors and dealing with war matters, Lincoln and his wife attended a play at Ford's Theatre. This was a public performance and many people were very excited that the President would be in the audience. They were given their own 'box' — a private balcony area — where Lincoln could sit in a rocking chair and watch in comfort. A police officer named John Parker was assigned to stand at the door that led from the hallway into the box and prevent anyone from disturbing the President. Halfway through the play, for his own reasons, Parker left his post, leaving the area unguarded. This was just the opportunity actor John Wilkes Booth had been waiting for.

Although born in Maryland, Booth felt sympathy for the Confederate cause. Despite this, he had not enlisted in the Confederate Army. He felt guilty because he had not defended the South and now wanted to redeem himself. While Lincoln was busy watching the play, Booth crashed through the door of Lincoln's box and shot the President in the back of his head. He then leapt from the box onto the stage below, planning to escape through the side door of the theatre where he had a horse waiting. As Booth leapt, his heel caught in the Union flag that hung from the balcony, and he broke his leg as he landed. He still managed to escape through the stage door, however, and fled on horseback, leaving the theatre in chaos.

A doctor tried to revive Lincoln, but by morning he was dead.

Booth rode south into Virginia, expecting to be welcomed as a hero by the Virginians, but no one wanted to help him and he was turned away. Twelve days later, Union soldiers finally found him, hiding in a barn, on a farm near the Rappahannock River. The soldiers set the barn on fire to drive him out, and shot him as he came to the door.

Emancipation and reconstruction

With Lincoln dead, Vice-President Andrew Johnson became the new President. Johnson set about completing reconstruction, but he did not possess the same beliefs as Lincoln. He was not against slavery, but he did feel that freed slaves worked harder and liberation could therefore be economically valuable. In December 1865, eight months after Lincoln's death, the United States passed the Thirteenth Amendment to the Constitution, which outlawed slavery. Johnson declared that states which agreed to this amendment would be welcomed back into the Union.

Although the Constitution now said that slaves were to be freed, the government did little to help them after their liberation. Freed slaves were neither given land where they could live nor payment for the years they had spent working for their masters. They left slavery with nothing, and now had to earn a living in a hostile environment. Many were forced to work on farms owned by white farmers who were bitter because their slaves had been taken away. These free black men and women were often treated just as badly as they had been while enslaved.

As Johnson did not think slavery was morally wrong, he did not feel much sympathy for the plight of the former slaves and was reluctant to see them get civil rights or full citizenship. This period was known as the 'tragic era', as freed slaves in the South were not allowed to benefit fully from their emancipation. A poll tax was levied which most of them could not afford. Failure to pay meant losing your right to vote. A 'grandfather clause' was introduced, which stated that men whose grandfathers had been slaves were ineligible to vote anyway. This potentially prevented many free blacks from voting for several generations. Finally, a literacy test required voters to explain the meaning of a legal document. Poor reading skills therefore also denied many uneducated former slaves the vote.

Strict 'black codes' were introduced, which meant that black people could not own guns, could only own property in the 'black' part of town and could not testify in court. They could be arrested for being 'impudent' to whites, or for not having a job.

A secret society called the Ku Klux Klan was formed in Tennessee in December 1865 with the aim of preventing blacks from gaining equal rights. It was a brutal organisation which spread terror in the South for five years, through whipping, burning, rape and murder. Klan members hid their identity beneath white masks and cloaks, and were often former confederate soldiers. The white police frequently did little or nothing to prevent these dreadful crimes or punish their perpetrators.

The Klan was outlawed in 1872, but many people still belonged secretly.

As part of reconstruction, a new agricultural system known as 'sharecropping' was developed. Plantation owners divided their properties and allowed both black and white people to work the land. In exchange, a percentage of the grown crop would be given to the landowner. This did provide some help for the ex-slaves but, as workers had to sell their crop to make any money, they often found themselves in debt and certainly not in a position to buy their own land.

Many northern businessmen moved south to take advantage of the financial opportunities now available. Southerners were very resentful of their arrival and referred to them as 'carpet-baggers' as they often carried carpet bags — a common form of luggage at the time. Some carpet-baggers joined together with freed slaves and were able to gain some power in the South, especially as so many southerners had lost their right to vote through refusing to agree to reconstruction. Southern whites who supported reconstruction, and allied themselves, were known derogatorily as 'scalawags'.

Johnson's opinions on slavery caused a lot of arguments within the government, and he was forced to agree to some changes. The Fourteenth Amendment to the Constitution was proclaimed in 1868, which extended federal legal protection equally to *all* citizens, regardless of race.

The former Union general, Ulysses S. Grant, was elected President in 1869. He continued with the Reconstruction Plan and with trying to appease both the North and South. In 1870, Grant signed the Naturalization Act, allowing all people of African descent living in the United States to become citizens. The Fifteenth Amendment was also made, abolishing racial restrictions on voting. State land in the South was opened up to black citizens, and the 'Freedman's Bureau' (set up in 1865) operated hospitals and schools for them. By 1874, around a fifth of black citizens were literate.

Although the federal government had given black people rights, each state was still able to make its own laws. Between the years 1890 and 1910, a series of 'Jim Crow' laws — named after a racist song called 'Jump Jim Crow' — were passed by the state governments in the South. These discriminated further against black citizens, encouraged segregation and ensured that black men and women were treated as second class citizens. Under these laws, they were prevented from using the same public facilities, restaurants, hotels and theatres as whites, and from living in the same areas. Marriage between black and white people became illegal in some states. Segregation in the armed services, which began during the Civil War, became normal. Jim Crow laws still applied in many southern states as late as 1954.

The Civil War had ended slavery but, for many, it brought little or no improvement to life.

Revision

Why was there a civil war in the United States?

To what extent did slavery cause the civil war?

— disagreement over slavery caused a division between the North and South but was not the only reason war was declared

— population increase in the North meant that it had more power in government and the South felt they were not fairly represented

— the North wanted tariffs on imported goods to help protect their new industries

— the North also wanted taxes on exported goods

— both harmed the Southern States by damaging their overseas trade.

What was the significance of Lincoln's election as President?

— Lincoln was elected as the North had more representation in government

— he was against slavery and wanted to remove individual state rights on this issue

— his election triggered states leaving the Union.

Why was the North able to win the war?

— the North had a larger established army

— northern industry was able to provide equipment for the war

— the North had better railways and could move their troops faster

— it had a navy which it used to blockade southern supplies

— Lincoln's Emancipation Proclamation prevented other countries from joining in.

Did the war change anything?

— amendments to the Constitution abolished slavery, gave federal legal protection to all and extended voting rights

— reforms took a long time to implement

— for a long time after their emancipation, many slaves received no help and found themselves in a situation that was no better, and sometimes worse

— the 'black codes' and 'Jim Crow Laws' maintained and legitimized segregation between black and white citizens.

Some questions for you to try

1   What was the Compromise of 1850?

2   Describe the events at Harper's Ferry in 1859.

3   What was the Dred Scott decision?

4   How different were the lifestyles and outlook of the northern and southern states in the years before the Civil War? Explain your answer.

5   Why was slavery an issue in American politics before the Civil War?

6   How did southerners justify slavery?

7   How did northern states deal with runaway slaves, and those attempting to escape, in the 1850s?

8   Why were the southern states alarmed by the election of Lincoln as President?

9   'The American Civil War was not about slavery.' How far do you agree with this statement? Explain your answer.

10 Why did Lincoln issue the Emancipation Proclamation?

11 To what extent were black Americans better off as a result of the Civil War? Explain your answer.

12 What were the aims of reconstruction after the American Civil War?

13 How far was reconstruction a success? Explain your answer.

14 Was the Civil War a disaster for the South? Explain your answer.

Chapter 6

European imperialism

6.1 The British Empire

In the mid-18th century, Britain was a major trading nation, and its goods were traded across the world by companies such as the East India Company and the Hudson's Bay Company. Trading posts provided good opportunities for the sale of British goods abroad and the ability to buy produce unavailable in Britain, such as cotton and tea. But at this time Britain did not possess much territory abroad (with the exception of that in America, which was lost in 1783). By 1900, things had changed; Britain had a huge empire which covered a quarter of the world's land mass.

The growth of the British Empire was largely due to the competition for resources and markets, which had existed for several hundred years, between England and her rivals: Spain, France, and The Netherlands. During the reign of Elizabeth I, England set up trading companies in Turkey, Russia and the East Indies, and explored the coast of North America, establishing colonies, which grew.

There had always been competition between the European powers for land, wealth, power and status, and overseas territories offered all four of these. The French, Dutch, Spanish, Portuguese and Germans all took land overseas, but Britain had the strongest navy and was able to claim the most.

Between 1700 and 1850, Britain fought a number of wars, which brought more colonies, as prizes for victory: Gibraltar was won in the War of Spanish Succession

The British Empire at its peak

(1701-1714); Canada and parts of India were gained after defeating France and Austria in the Seven Years War (1756-63); Sri Lanka and parts of South Africa were gained at the end of the Napoleonic Wars (1799-1815). In addition, Singapore was acquired in 1819 after negotiations with the Sultan, James Cook claimed Australia, and New Zealand signed the Waitangi treaty.

During the 18th century, most British politicians thought that having an empire was a bad idea as running colonies abroad was very expensive, and they required protection. However, these attitudes began to change when the benefits of controlling land overseas became more apparent.

Countries within the British Empire were treated as British possessions, and there were strict trade rules. They were not allowed to sell their goods to other European nations, and could only use British ships to carry their goods. The British Navy guarded the oceans so that those goods could be shipped safely to ports around the globe. Britain's trade boomed and huge docks had to be built at her ports to handle all the produce. Cheap raw materials such as sugar, cotton, cocoa and tea were imported and processed in British factories, then either resold in Britain or exported. Foreign foods, such as bananas, could be transported in refrigerated ships, creating an exciting new diet for the wealthy.

With the advantages recognised, British banks loaned the money needed to build factories, mines, and railways in British colonies throughout the world.

In 1851, proud of their great empire, Queen Victoria and Prince Albert hosted 'The Great Exhibition of the Works of Industry of All Nations'. Countries from all across the world were invited to bring their inventions, their machines, and their goods to this fair. 'The Crystal Palace' — an enormous glass building — was constructed to house the exhibition. Thousands of objects were put on display for the millions of visitors to admire. Half the exhibits came from within the British Empire, promoting it as the greatest empire in the world and as powerful as the rest of the world put together.

The colonies may have been valuable resources, but many British people thought that the colonists benefitted from the Empire as well. The British believed themselves the superior race in the world and that the colonial peoples could learn from the 'mother country' and improve themselves. With Britain's help they could learn about modern developments in science, technology and medicine. Millions of people left Britain and went to live all over the Empire, some willingly and some forcibly transported. Many went as missionaries to spread Christianity to the 'heathen' natives of the new territories.

Britain may have led the way, but other European nations followed close behind. Soon France, The Netherlands, Spain, Portugal, Belgium, Italy, Germany, Austria-Hungary and Russia were all making claims on land and expanding their empires.

Europeans and Americans were eager to read of adventures on distant shores. Newspapers competed for readership by hiring reporters to search the globe for stories set in mysterious unfamiliar places.

Revision

Why did Europeans take over much of the world in the 19th century?

What had been the impact of imperialism by the start of the 19th century?

— Britain was a major trading nation with trading posts and colonies all over the world

— overseas territories had been gained through war and exploration

— rivalry between European nations led to more territory claimed

— there was a desire to trade in goods unavailable within Europe.

How did imperialism develop during the 19th century?

— Britain's Empire expanded to cover a quarter of the globe

— the value of overseas colonies and the financial rewards they brought were recognised

— European countries all wanted to be the most powerful and fought to control as much land as possible.

What social, political, military, economic and religious factors encouraged imperialism?

— there was a growing interest in new places and reading about their discovery

— the industrial revolution and the consequent development of weapons meant that European countries had the means to overpower others

— a larger Empire meant a larger military resource in times of conflict

— colonies brought a larger and cheaper labour force

— the desire to spread Christianity to 'heathen' natives

— colonies brought wealth and power for the controlling nation

— new and exotic foods could be imported

— control of trade routes brought financial rewards.

How was imperialism justified at the time?

— British and other European people thought themselves superior and felt it their duty to spread their knowledge and ideas

— 'civilisation' was being shared with the natives

— Christianity was being spread

— money was being made.

Some questions for you to try

1   What is meant by 'imperialism'?

2   Why was there a growth in European imperialism in the 19th century?

3   Why was it considered important for missionaries to spread Christianity?

4   What do you think was the main motive behind western imperialism?

5   How far do you think imperialism benefitted the native populations abroad?

6.2 Imperialism in China

Britain attempts trade with China

During the second half of the 18th century, Emperor Qianlong of the Qing Dynasty reigned over China. While nations in the west had developed, modernised and built colonies around the world, Qianlong had looked on without interest. Western ideas about equality and liberty did not seem relevant to China. Qianlong did not send ambassadors abroad, build trading ships or allow western merchants to roam through his country. As far as he was concerned, China had everything its people could ever desire.

Qianlong made it illegal for the British to import their products into China and demanded that all goods sold to foreigners be purchased in silver coin or bullion. This particularly annoyed the British as they had to buy this from Europe before they could trade with China, making it very expensive. The Emperor also declared that foreign ships could only come to one Chinese port — the port of Guangzhou (which the British called Canton) — and that foreigners who came to trade there would

have to follow strict regulations. For example: no foreign women were allowed to visit the dock; no foreign merchant was allowed to speak directly to a Chinese official, without an interpreter; and none could remain in China after trading.

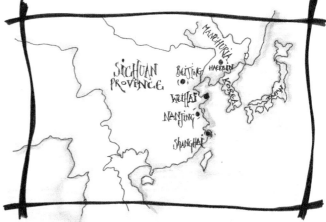

The Chinese may have felt that they did not need Europe, but Europe, and in particular Britain, needed China. The British wanted the Chinese silks and spices that were unavailable in Europe, as well as the tea. They loved their tea, huge quantities of which were imported every year from China.

The British felt annoyed that they were only allowed to trade at one port, and that they were spending huge amounts of silver coin and bullion in China while the Chinese were buying nothing in return.

George III sent an ambassador, George Macartney, to China in 1793 to ask Emperor Qianlong to change their trade regulations. Qianlong did not receive ambassadors, however, as that would mean accepting that other kings were as important as he was. As far as Qianlong was concerned, foreign visitors only came to his court to pay tribute. Macartney was not permitted to visit Qianlong at his palace inside the Forbidden City, and a meeting was instead arranged in a yurt outside the city walls. He brought with him a whole ship full of British merchandise to show the emperor what wonderful products Britain had to trade, but the Emperor treated this as a gift. He had everything sent to his Summer Palace and saw Macartney without the goods. All that Macartney had left to give the Emperor was a letter from King George III explaining that Britain wanted to send an ambassador to China to live in Peking, access to all of China's ports and permission to build trading posts. The Emperor refused.

The First Opium War

The British were angered by the Emperor's decision. They needed to find something that the Chinese could not refuse to buy from them. The answer was opium.

Opium was a drug made from poppy juice, pressed into tablets or stirred into syrup. British doctors gave it to patients who were in pain and it had been used in China for medicinal purposes for around five hundred years. Opium not only took away pain, it also made patients feel peaceful and serene and sometimes caused hallucinations that could last for days. Many people liked this feeling and the use of opium as a recreational drug was spreading in Britain. Unfortunately, it had other side effects too. It made patients feel very confused and was highly addictive. Addicts became known as 'opium-eaters'. The more they took, the less effective it became, and the more they needed to take to achieve the desired state. Quitting was almost impossible and withdrawal symptoms included distress, anxiety and deep depression.

The British East India Company grew poppies in India, where the juice was made into opium and packed onto ships, ready to be exported. The British sent some of these ships to China and sold opium at the port of Canton. They smuggled it into other ports as well. The Chinese who bought the opium smoked it, which made the effect even stronger.

When the Emperor learned of how his people were being drugged, and of the amount of money that was suddenly leaving China, he was very angry and made opium illegal. He banned all British ships from bringing it into China. The Emperor expected his word to be followed, but the British ignored his demands and carried on shipping opium in secret. Corrupt Chinese officials continued to let it through.

At last, the British were making money from Chinese trade whether the Emperor liked it or not.

British officials in India could see how much money they could earn by growing poppies, and did their best to send more opium to China. Initially, only the rich had been able to afford it but, with so much being sent, the price decreased, allowing ordinary people to buy it too. In 'opium dens' all over China, addicts lay on mats, smoking and drifting into a dreamlike state. Meanwhile, the British Empire tried to ban its subjects from taking the drug as they could see the negative effects it had.

In the last years of his reign, Emperor Qianlong gave more and more power to his advisor, Heshen. He even allowed him to marry one of his daughters. Qianlong relied on Heshen and trusted his judgement, but many of the other court officials could see that Heshen was corrupt and happy to take bribes.

In 1796, at the end of his sixtieth year as Emperor, Qianlong passed the title to his fifth son, Jiaqing. He felt it was disrespectful to rule any longer than his ancestor, who had ruled for sixty-one years. However, Jiaqing did not actually get to rule until his father died, four years later. When he eventually gained control, one of the first things he did was arrest Heshen and give him permission to commit honourable suicide.

Jiaqing had inherited a very unstable and unhappy empire. His staff lived very well, but the people were paying heavy taxes to fund this lifestyle and the treasury was almost empty. He tried to reorganise the government but there were so many dishonest officials that it was almost impossible. When he died in 1820, he was the most hated Emperor of his dynasty, and the government was still just as corrupt.

The new Emperor, Daoguang, was left with the problem of a corrupt and bankrupt government, as well as that of opium. By now, more people than ever were addicted to the drug, and thousands of chests of opium were being smuggled into China every year. The Chinese had spent so much on opium that the country had run out of money. Daoguang appointed Lin Zexu as the new governor of Canton, whose main task was to reduce and eventually eliminate the opium trade. Lin Zexu immediately sent orders for sixty of the biggest opium dealers to be arrested. He then sent a message to the British ships anchored in Canton ordering all opium on every ship to be handed over, or no trade of any sort would be allowed ever again. Any British merchant found trading opium from now on would be arrested and put to death. He closed the channel into Canton, to prevent any ship from leaving, and gave the merchants one night to make a decision.

By morning the harbour was covered in posters repeating the deal and thousands of Chinese soldiers filled the docks. The British Chief Superintendent of Trade in China, Charles Elliot, managed to convince the merchants to hand over their opium stock, with the promise of eventual compensation for their loss by the British Government. Twenty thousand chests were given up and thrown into the sea on June 3rd 1839 — so much that it took *three weeks* to all wash away.

Having dealt with the immediate problem, Lin Zexu wrote to Queen Victoria requesting she support the Chinese in stopping the trade in opium as it had 'poisoned' thousands of Chinese civilians. The message apparently never reached her.

After this incident, the atmosphere grew tense between the Chinese and British merchants. At the end of June, the Chinese coastguard in Kowloon arrested the commodore of the *Carnatic,* a British clipper. The reasons surrounding his arrest are unclear. A few days later, in Kowloon, a large group of British and American sailors, including crew from the *Carnatic,* were drinking rice liquor and getting out of control. A riot started, and the sailors vandalised a temple and killed a man. The Chinese government ordered the men handed over, but the British refused. Because China did not offer trial by jury, the British government demanded that the men by tried in a British court. Six of the sailors were prosecuted by the British authorities in Canton, but then sent back to England as free men.

The Chinese were furious and insisted that British merchants could now only trade if they signed a bond, under penalty of death, promising not to smuggle opium, agreeing to Chinese laws and acknowledging Chinese jurisdiction. Charles Elliot refused to sign the bonds and ordered all British traders out of Canton, banning them from trading in China. He hoped the Chinese would back down, with the threat of losing all British trade, but some merchants, who were not dealing in opium, weakened the British position by independently signing the bond.

In London, the British government was angered and decided to teach the Chinese a lesson by preventing these independent merchants from trading with them. When British merchant ships tried to trade, the British navy warships stepped in to blockade the port of Canton refusing to let any ships enter or leave. The Chinese had no comparable navy and were powerless to do anything about it.

The blockade lasted for four years, until eventually, in 1843, the Chinese surrendered and signed the Treaty of Nanjing (the 'Unequal Treaty'). This gave Great Britain everything she wanted and China nothing; the Chinese even had to pay for the opium they had thrown into the sea. They had to agree to open up five more ports for British trade, allow English merchants to build settlements and live in China all year round, and give up the island of Hong Kong. If this was not bad enough for China, other countries saw what the British had done and threatened the same.

Soon similar treaties with France and America had been signed.

The Second Opium War

For twelve years an uneasy truce held as more and more European traders entered China, but it was not to last. In October 1856, Chinese officials arrested the crew of the *Arrow*, a Chinese-owned ship, registered in Hong Kong. The crew were arrested under suspicion of involvement in piracy and smuggling. Despite the fact they were all Chinese, British officials demanded their release, claiming that, because the ship had recently been British-registered, it was protected under the Treaty of Nanjing. The British insisted that the *Arrow* had been flying a British ensign and that Chinese soldiers had insulted the flag by boarding the ship. The Chinese insisted that the ship was not flying the flag when they boarded it and that they were within their rights to arrest their own sailors. The matter did not drop and the British continued to insist that all sailors were 'returned', with a letter of apology.

The Chinese eventually agreed.

As it happened, the registration of the *Arrow* had expired, and so no British flag would have been flying when the sailors were arrested.

Following this, several documents, each known as a 'Treaty of Tientsin', were signed in June 1858. The British, French, Russians and Americans were all involved. These forced the reluctant Chinese to open more ports to foreigners, permitted foreign ambassadors in Beijing, allowed Christian missionaries into China and legalised the opium trade. A separate treaty was also signed with Russia giving it land in Manchuria.

In June 1859, an Anglo-French naval force, with over two thousand troops on more than twenty ships, sailed to Beijing, bringing envoys for a new embassy. Angry at having been forced to sign the treaties, the Chinese blocked the river, preventing the ships from passing. British forces blew up the iron obstacles and sailed on, attacking the nearby Fort of Taku as they went. The furious Chinese, determined not to let them reach their destination, fought back, managing to force the ships to retreat. Their victory was short lived, however; more troops were sent the following summer.

More than one hundred and seventy ships loaded with soldiers sailed from Hong Kong to Beijing and landed just three miles from the fort. Once again, the Chinese fought the invaders, but this time they were not strong enough. After three weeks of fighting, the British and French captured the fort and sailed on to Beijing to start building their embassy.

The situation was very tense; the current Emperor Xianfeng dispatched ministers for peace talks, but any hope of resolution broke down when British envoy, Harry Parkes, was wrongly arrested. Parkes was marking out the British camp, in the area previously agreed, when he and his men were imprisoned and interrogated. Some were murdered by 'slow slicing', where parts of the body are sliced off with a knife, a bit at a time to prolong the agony, sometimes with torture devices applied. The result was a slow and painful death, which often left the body unrecognizable. Furious at this treatment, the British and French let leash their full wrath on the Chinese army, virtually destroying it.

With the army devastated, the Emperor fled the city, leaving his brother Prince Gong in charge of negotiations. British and French troops freed Parkes and the remaining prisoners. The troops entered the Forbidden City and looted the Emperor's Summer Palace and Old Summer Palace. For three days they were ransacked. Both were virtually destroyed, although the Summer Palace was rebuilt in 1886. The destruction of the Forbidden City was also discussed, but never carried out.

The 'Self-Strengthening Movement'

China's Empire was weak and the Emperor powerless. Other European countries took advantage of her weakness and seized territory. Soon China was full of foreigners and missionaries from all over Europe and its people were learning all about the ways of the West, whether they wanted to or not. With all this foreign influence, the Chinese government began to think that it would, after all, be beneficial to learn about western ideas and technology; then they would stand a chance of becoming equal.

The Chinese learnt about western weapons and strengthened their army. They learned about boat building and strengthened their navy. Coal mines, iron works, and textile mills were opened, increasing production. Railways were built and telegraph lines erected to improve communication. Education was improved. In 1872, one hundred and twenty Chinese school boys were chosen to go to America to study western ideas. Thirty set out in August, with three more groups planned over the next three years. They were to stay for *fifteen years*. All expenses were paid by the Chinese government, in the belief that, when these boys returned, they would be able to help create a China that was strong enough to stand alongside the now dominant western countries. The boys settled in well with their new life and experienced freedoms they did not have in China.

Despite these efforts, the Self-Strengthening Movement was not as successful as it could have been. Western technology flooded an otherwise undeveloped country. Soldiers were not trained to use the new weapons, coal mines were inefficient and railways only covered a fraction of the land. Even the education in America proved unsuccessful; after just nine years, all the students were ordered back to China. It was felt they were learning too many western ideas and not enough about Chinese traditions. The program did open channels for diplomatic relations, so it was not a complete disaster.

The Boxer Rebellion

While China had been modernising, more and more European countries had crept into China. Many Chinese were unhappy about all these invaders, but none more so than a small group of Chinese rebels who formed a secret society aimed at evicting foreigners. This society was made up of men and women who were extremely loyal to their country, but who thought their government was not doing a very good job. It called itself 'Yihtuan', meaning 'Society of Righteous and Harmonious Fists', but they soon became known as the 'Yihe Magic Boxers', or just 'Boxers' for short, because of their great skill in the martial arts.

The Boxers were a nationalist group, who believed that foreigners were evil and devilish. They hated Christians and any Chinese who worked with foreigners. The Boxers were very superstitious and believed they could conjure up the spirits of their ancestors to help them in battle and that these 'spirit soldiers' would make them immune to western bullets. They used incantations and spells to put themselves into a trance when they believed their bodies could be possessed.

The first attacks were made against German missionaries. Germany had sent hundreds of missionaries into the centre of China to spread Christianity. This made them very unpopular with the Chinese; many were attacked and killed. Chinese friends of the missionaries were also killed.

The Boxers continued their attacks, and the government of China did little to stop them. The Emperor, Guangxu, disapproved of the violence, but many court officials felt differently, including Guangxu's aunt Cixi, the Dowager Empress. When Guangxu, had first become emperor he made himself very unpopular, very quickly. He had tried to make several changes to the way China was run, in an attempt to modernise the country, but to many Chinese people, modernisation meant westernisation, so Guangxu was disliked. When Cixi saw how unpopular her nephew was becoming, she raised at army against him and took power for herself. With attacks getting out of control, governments from around the world ordered Cixi to stop the rebels. She agreed but never ordered her army to act.

As the rebellion grew, many foreigners in China fled to their embassies in Beijing, seeking refuge in the walled section of the city called the 'legation compound'. Still Cixi took no action, and the Boxers surrounded the embassies. Cixi now declared that China was at war with the countries of the West.

News of the siege soon reached the rest of the world and soldiers from several different nations prepared to march into Beijing to rescue the prisoners. Thousands of soldiers from Russia, Japan, America, Britain and France landed on the shores of China and marched towards Beijing.

The Boxers went out to meet them, convinced that the special charms they wore and the words they recited would make them invincible. The western soldiers opened fire on the Boxers. The charms did not work. They broke down the gates of the Forbidden City, where the Chinese Government had its headquarters, invaded the city and once again attacked the Summer Palace. Cixi, fearful for her life, dressed herself as a peasant, collected her nephew and fled in an old cart.

Chinese government officials were left to try and calm the situation. They promised that, if the western soldiers left China, they would ensure the Boxers were properly dealt with. They insisted that Cixi's declaration of war had not been official and agreed to punish those who had supported the rebellion. They also promised to build stronger walls around the legation compound, repair the railways which had been destroyed in the fighting and pay compensation.

The West agreed but had some terms of their own to add. Cixi was allowed to return as Empress Dowager, but she had to agree that schools would now teach western ideas, that foot binding would be outlawed and that she would send officials abroad to learn about the constitution and government of European countries.

Three years later in 1908, Cixi died of a stroke. Her nephew, Guangxu, died shortly afterwards in suspicious circumstances, possibly poisoned as his aunt's dying wish.

Cixi's chosen heir was the three-year-old Prince Puyi. Too young to rule, Puyi lived a life of luxury inside the Forbidden City, protected from the real world. Puyi was treated like a little god and never even saw another child until he was seven. Qing noblemen were supposed to run China for him, but in reality they just did whatever Russia, Japan and the United States told them to do.

The Sichuan Rebellion

In 1911, officials in the Sichuan Province wanted to build their own railway — a railway that would belong to China, not a foreign country. Many Sichuan merchants had given money to help with construction, but it was not enough. The Qing regents announced they would take over but, to finish the job, their government needed to make a deal with European bankers. This meant that the Sichuan railway would no longer belong just to the Chinese. Horrified, the officials refused to hand over the project and announced that they would no longer obey either the Qing regents or the Qing government. Instead, they would set up a new Chinese republic, with its own government. The capital would be the city of Nanjing and the president a doctor called Sun Yat-sen.

Sun Yat-sen had tried to lead a rebellion against the Qing dynasty in 1895, sixteen years before, but his plans were discovered and he had to flee. He spent time in Japan and Europe, but had now returned and was ready to lead the revolutionaries who called themselves the 'Kuomintang' — the Nationalist Party.

The Sichuan rebellion spread all over China. The Qing regents knew they could not oppose the will of the people or fight the armed members of the Nationalist Party. In February 1912, Puyi abdicated, ending the Qing dynasty. China was flooded with western ideas and, for the first time in thousands of years, found itself without an emperor.

Revision

What was the nature and impact of 19th century imperialism in China?

What was Chinese society like in the early 19th century?

— the Qing Emperor ruled the country

— the Chinese felt they had everything they needed and did not want western influence

— they were not interested in learning about Christianity

— they were making a lot of money selling Chinese goods, but bought nothing in return

— they refused the building of foreign trading posts and allowed trade in only one port

— they wanted foreigners in China to abide by Chinese rules and regulations.

How did western countries extend their influence in China in the 19th century?

— the British smuggled opium into China

— westerners refused to follow Chinese rules

— missionaries were sent to teach the Chinese about Christianity

— western powers used their military strength to force treaties

— the West used weapons and warships the Chinese did not have

— the West combined their forces to overpower the Chinese army and rebel groups.

How did the Chinese react to European intervention?

— they initially tried to fight back

— they decided to learn from the West to make China as strong

— rebel groups fought against foreign influence.

How significant was the impact of western intervention for China?

— the Imperial family and government became answerable to the West

— the Emperor eventually lost all power

— traditional Chinese customs were abolished

— western ideas were taught in Chinese schools.

Some questions for you to try

1   Why did European countries want to trade in China?

2   Was the opium trade responsible for the downfall of the Imperial family?

3   Which had the larger effect on China: the Self-Strengthening Movement or the Boxer Rebellion?

4   How damaging was the The Treaty of Nanjing to the people of China?

5   Was the Self-Strengthening Movement a complete failure?

6   Was the Boxer Rebellion a complete failure?

6.3 Imperialism in India

The British annexe India

In the 17th century, India was a huge and wealthy nation, but the 18th century saw a succession of weak emperors who were given bad advice and made poor decisions. Fighting took place with neighbouring nations and within India itself, weakening, bankrupting and dividing the country. There was still an emperor, but he held very little power. Instead, India was controlled by numerous individuals, each ruling a separate regional state.

While all this had been going on, the British East India Company had been establishing trading posts. After it gained permission from the Emperor to build these in the late 17th century, individual rulers were often willing to make independent deals, and trade grew rapidly.

India had many things the British wanted — in particular: saltpetre, indigo dye, cotton, silk and opium — but the chaos there worried them. In order to protect their traders and trading posts, they decided to build fortified walls around them in Bombay and in Bengal. The governor of Bengal, Siraj Ud Daulah, was horrified and angered to see the British building 'Fort William' in the Bengali settlement of Calcutta, and placing guns along its walls, without even asking his permission.

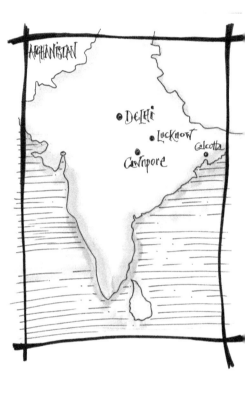

Siraj was determined to teach the British a lesson and show them who was in charge, but was not sure that his Bengal army could defeat them unaided. He offered the French land if they would help him chase the British out of Calcutta. The French also had trading posts in India and were delighted at the prospect of not only gaining more land, but of beating an old enemy too.

The combined forces of Bengal and France marched towards Calcutta. Fort William was barely finished, and only a few soldiers stood on its walls. Siraj's army was able to capture it after less than four days. On June 19th 1756, his men poured in and he ordered all captives to be thrown into its dungeon, 'the black hole'. The prisoners were left all night in suffocating conditions, without food or water. By morning, most of them had died.

The British were furious at being treated this way and the East India Company took drastic measures to avenge the deaths. It hired its own army and sent it to punish Siraj and the population of Bengal. A private company hiring an army to invade a country because its workers were badly treated was something previously unheard of.

Sir Robert Clive, general of the East India Company army, marched his men to meet those of the Governor. However, Clive was not prepared to take any chances. He made a pact with the senior enemy general, Mir Jafar, promising he could become the new ruler of Bengal if he betrayed Siraj.

When the Indian army met the East India Company at the Battle of Plassey, Mir Jafar surrendered without a fight. The Bengal soldiers, having no instruction, panicked and started to retreat. Siraj was killed and Clive kept his promise; he announced that Mir Jafar was the new 'naweb' (ruler) of Bengal.

Mir Jafar may have been given the title he wanted, but he owed his position to the British and they made sure he did not forget it. He had to do whatever they wanted him to do or face being overthrown. When he finally did resist its orders, the East India Company simply sent its army to remove him. Mir Jafar became known as a traitor throughout India.

With no naweb, the East India Company decided *they* would rule Bengal, and declared Calcutta its capital. For a while, the British continued to follow India's laws and traditions but, as time when on, this began to change. The Emperor was now unable to do anything about it.

Over the following years, the Indian empire continued to fall apart and the East India Company claimed more and more land. Eventually it took the Emperor himself under its 'protection'. The Emperor of India had to do exactly as the East India Company told him.

The Company used a system of Direct Rule to control the country, making laws that benefited its trade, and forcing the Indian people to comply. The British wanted to modernise India and impose western ideas. Temples were torn down to make room for railway tracks and Christian missionaries taught throughout the country. Traditional Hindu and Muslim practices were discouraged and many felt that their faith was threatened.

Lord William Bentinck became Governor of Bengal in 1827, and wanted to make the East India Company even more profitable. He introduced several cost cutting measures, including cutting the wages of the soldiers and reformed the court system, making English the language used. He encouraged western education and was involved in the banning of 'suttee' (also, 'sati'), when a widow would be burnt alive on her husband's funeral pyre. His interference in cultural traditions made him very unpopular among the Indian people. There were even rumours that he planned to demolish the Taj Mahal and sell the marble. He actually *did* sell marble from Agra Fort, an important Indian monument, and metal from the Agra Gun, a historical artefact and the largest cannon ever cast.

In 1848, James Broun-Ramsay, Marquess of Dalhousie was appointed Governor-General of India. Dalhousie was a hard worker and set about trying to expand the Empire and extend modernisation. He oversaw the continued development of railways, roads, postal services and the telegraph, which further upset the Indian people. He was also responsible for adding the Punjab and parts of Burma (now, Myanmar) to the list of British-controlled territories. One of Dalhousie's most controversial policies was his 'Doctrine of Lapse'. This policy declared that if the ruler of any state under the influence of the East India Company lacked a natural heir then it would be annexed to the British Empire. Under this rule, Dalhousie gained several territories and became still more unpopular.

The Sepoy Mutiny

By 1856, the East India Company had three large armies which they used to control the millions in India. The officers were all British, but many of the soldiers were Indian. These Indian soldiers were called 'sepoys'.

The British passed a law in 1856 declaring that any soldier who belonged to the British army in India could be put on a ship and sent to fight in another country in times of conflict. At this time the British had just finished fighting in the Crimea, and the possibility of being called upon to fight abroad was very real. Hindu soldiers were horrified. A Hindu believes that he can only keep himself clean if he cooks his own food and draws his own bath. This would be impossible aboard a ship. A Hindu soldier who went on a British ship could find that his relatives and friends refused to eat with him because he was tainted. Muslims were also shocked. They followed daily rituals, with which such a venture would interfere. To make matters worse, the East India Company had also bought the new, modern 'Pattern 1853' (P53) Enfield rifle for its soldiers to use. To operate this rifle, a soldier was required to bite off the end of each cartridge before loading it. These cartridges contained grease made from animal fat. Muslims do not eat anything from a pig as they consider them unclean, and Hindus will not eat anything from a cow as they consider them to be sacred, and so neither wished to use the new rifles. The sepoys felt that adopting the P53 Enfield was a deliberate attempt by the East India Company to destroy their faith and decided to rebel against them. In an attempt to unite Muslims and Hindus, they declared the Emperor their leader and that they would no longer follow the British.

The Emperor at this time, Bahadur Shah II, was eighty-two and too old to fight, but he announced his support for the rebels and watched as they attacked the cities of Delhi, Cawnpore and Lucknow. In retaliation, the East India Company hired more British soldiers and laid siege to Delhi. The sepoys fought hard to keep hold of the city, but the Company army was too strong and soon retook it. Bahadur Shah surrenderd and was put on trial for treason. He was found guilty and sent to live in exile under guard. He died five years later, at the age of eighty-seven.

The Raj

After the death of Bahadur Shah, the British decided that India would no longer have an emperor. The British government also decided that the East India Company had made too many mistakes and should no longer rule either. The Government of India Act was passed in 1858, transferring control of India to the Crown. Queen Victoria announced that India was now a kingdom (raj) of the British Empire, ruled by her and governed directly by Parliament.

With the rebellion over, the British continued to force western ideas, technology and laws on India. They introduced dams, irrigation schemes, factories, hospitals, schools, clinics and universities, all based on British ideas. Despite these 'improvements', India remained extremely poor and was hit by famine on several occasions.

One true, and particularly significant, improvement the British made was in actively dealing with 'Thuggee'. This referred to bands of robbers who befriended travellers before robbing and murdering them. There had been a long tradition of such behaviour in India, to which the British decided to put an end. By setting up a special police force to hunt them down, encouraging informants and warning travellers of the danger, the Thuggee cult was finally eradicated. Building railways also helped wipe it out as few people then travelled long distances on foot.

The British in India thought that they had a duty to bring their own customs and ways to India, because they believed that these were much better than Indian tradition. However, no matter how much they talked about the benefits for India, the Indian people could see clearly that whites had more privileges, more wealth and a better lifestyle than they did. British citizens lived in reserved neighbourhoods, where the only Indians were servants, nursemaids, cooks or nannies, who had to call a white man 'sahib' and a white woman 'memsahib', meaning master and mistress.

Indians did not want masters and mistresses; they wanted to rule their own country and to be treated as equals.

Revision

What was the nature and impact of 19th century imperialism in India?

What was British rule like before 1857?

— the Emperor had lost power and was under the 'protection' of the British

— each area of the country was ruled by local officials who were easily bribed

— missionaries spread Christian ideas, disregarding Hindu and Muslim traditions

— British trading posts and settlements were expanding and taking more and more land

— British laws and the English language were introduced in courts

— Indian traditions, like suttee (or sati), were banned

— the 'lapse and annexe' policy ensured additional territories fell under British control.

Why did rebellion against British rule occur in 1857, and why did it fail?

— sepoy soldiers were angered when told they could be forced to fight abroad and at the introduction of the Lee-Enfield rifle

— Muslims and Hindus felt the British were deliberately trying to destroy their faith

— the sepoys gave allegiance to the Emperor, but he was too old and inexperienced to lead an army

— the East India Company had the ability to hire more soldiers and overpower the rebels.

How much were British attitudes and the nature of their rule changed by the events of 1857?

— the Emperor was removed from power

— the Queen, rather than the East India Company now ruled India

— the British Government felt that the East India Company had treated the sepoys badly and that rebellion could have been avoided

— the British were even more determined to westernise India and allow it to benefit from their knowledge and experience

— Indian people were seen as inferior to the British.

How much was 19ᵗʰ century India changed by British rule?

— trade increased

— more British arrived in India and lived in reserved areas

— the Indian people became servants to very much wealthier English masters.

Some questions for you to try

1   What was the role of the East India Company in India?

2   Was Lord Dalhousie successful as Governor-General?

3   Why did the Indian Mutiny break out in 1857?

4   Did the sepoys stand any chance of winning against the British?.

5   Given that India was already weak and divided, did the British actually make things worse for the Indian people?

6   What was suttee (or sati)?

7   What was Thuggee?

8   Why did the British Government take control of India after the 1857 Mutiny?

6.4 Imperialism in Africa

The Scramble for Africa

Africa was a wild and mysterious land in the early 19th century, a place Europeans knew little about. The first Europeans to settle there were the Portuguese as early as the 15th century, followed closely by the Dutch. Other Europeans had previously travelled to Africa to buy and capture slaves, but had not stayed. The 19th century saw efforts made to explore and map this unknown area. David Livingstone, Henry Stanley and others travelled through the centre of Africa, discovering tens of thousands of square miles of land, containing new sources of wealth.

As far as Europeans were concerned, no one owned this land. It was there for the taking.

The value of overseas colonies was appreciated by the 19th century and advances in weaponry, communication and travel made it easy for European countries to claim territory and establish

them. France, Germany, Britain, Spain, Portugal, Belgium and Russia all saw the value of Africa and started building trading posts around the coast in order profit from rich resources, such as ivory, rubber, limestone, gold and silver.

King Leopold II of Belgium wanted his people to share in this wealth and tried to convince their parliament to claim the Congo basin. When it refused, he announced that instead he was going to found a new charity, the 'International African Association', which would bring modern science and trade to Africans. Leopold hired Henry Stanley to help him map out the required routes in the Congo and had trading posts and little medical offices built all along them, in the name of the Association. He then claimed all free land along the route for his own private, personal colony in Africa.

The Germans were next to grab huge areas of land in Africa. Under Bismarck's leadership, Germany had a plan of world expansion and aimed to take over as much territory as possible.

Other European countries did not wish to be left behind while Belgium and Germany took all the riches. Portugal, France, Italy and Britain were all soon laying claim to vast tracts.

The years after 1880 became known as the 'scramble', because so many countries were rushing to gain control of as much of Africa as they could. Every nation in Europe believed that whichever of them held the most foreign territory could claim to be the greatest power.

Europeans found land in Africa relatively easy to take as the natives had inferior weapons, were often willing to make deals and remained divided into tribes. African tribes were often preoccupied with fighting each other, leaving them open to exploitation.

The Berlin Conference

In 1884, Otto von Bismarck invited the rest of Europe to a conference in the German city of Berlin. Representatives from a dozen different countries met and decided that it would be best if they avoided fighting expensive wars over Africa. Instead, they would just divide it 'fairly'. If any country built trading posts and missionary stations in any part of Africa, that country could claim it and no other could claim or attack it. They also agreed to suppress the internal slave trade in Africa and ban importing fire arms there. The representatives all signed the agreement and went home, pleased with their civilized and peaceful solution.

The people who had lived in these areas for thousands of years were not so pleased.

Long before Europeans began deciding where new colonies and their borders were going to be, African tribes had been fighting wars and making alliances with each other. When the Europeans declared new borders, they often separated friendly tribes or locked together hostile ones.

Most Europeans thought Africans who lived in the plains and jungles were not fully human, and certainly not intelligent enough to rule. They believed they needed to be guided and controlled, like children, and not left to make decisions for themselves.

By 1900, every part of Africa, except Ethiopia and Liberia, had been claimed by a European country.

Rubber production

One of the main reasons Europeans wanted African land was cheap access to the natural resources it contained. In the now Belgian area of the Congo, rubber was a major resource, which came from wild vines in the jungle. In Brazil, rubber was collected by making a small cut in the tree and allowing the sticky sap to trickle out and be collected in a bucket. This method made harvesting it a slow process. The Belgians wanted a much quicker way of acquiring the rubber in the Congo. Here, the natives were ordered to slash the rubber plant and lather their bodies with the latex, which was left to set and then scraped from the skin. This was a painful process for the person concerned, whose body hair was often scraped away too. Collecting rubber this way was quick, but slashing the vines meant that they died. As a result, they soon became difficult to find. Despite this problem, the Belgium officials demanded an increase in the amount of rubber collected.

To ensure that the native population worked as hard as possible, a special organisation, known as the Force Publique (FP), was created to oversee rubber collection. The FP was made up of white Belgian officers of the State and both black and white soldiers. Many of the black soldiers had been kidnapped during raids on villages and raised in Roman Catholic missionaries, where they had been given military training in conditions no better than slavery.

It was the job of the FP to make sure that the natives were collecting enough rubber. Villagers who failed to meet their quota were punished and forced to pay the remaining amount in severed human hands. Sometimes the hands were collected by the soldiers of the Force Publique and sometimes by the villagers themselves. There were even small wars, where villages attacked each other to gather hands, since their rubber quotas were too unrealistic to fulfil. Anyone who protested against collecting rubber, or the cruel treatment, was punished by having their head cut off.

The brutality did not stop with overseeing rubber collection. Armed with modern weapons and a bull whip, the Force Publique routinely burned villages and imprisoned, tortured, flogged, raped and murdered native people. Officers were concerned that the soldiers might waste their ammunition on hunting animals for sport and so required soldiers to submit one hand for every bullet used. Each right hand collected by the FP was supposed to prove a killing. In practice, however, soldiers sometimes 'cheated' by simply cutting off the hand and leaving the victim to live or die. Survivors told stories of how they had lived through a massacre by pretending to be dead, not moving even when their hands were severed, and waiting till the soldiers left before seeking help.

In some instances a soldier could shorten his service term by bringing more hands than his peers. This led to widespread mutilation and dismemberment.

With the brutality of the FP, tribal wars, a lack of food and the introduction of new diseases, the native population of the Congo was almost halved during the period of Leopold's rule.

South Africa

While European countries scrambled for territory in the 19th century, South Africa had already been occupied by Europeans for over a hundred years.

Initially colonised by Dutch farmers ('Boers'), the southern tip of Africa had become a sought-after piece of land. Ever since the Boers had first settled in this area, the British had wanted it, and had made attempts to take it. After years of fights with the Dutch, the British finally claimed 'Cape Colony' in 1820. British settlers began to arrive and a new British governor took over.

The Boers hated life under British rule, particularly when Britain declared slavery illegal. The Dutch had always used slaves to work their fields and did not know how they were to manage without them. They also believed that God intended all black people to be slaves and refused to live in a colony where they would be living right beside whites, as free men and women.

The Great Trek of the Boers

Between 1835 and 1843, thousands of Boers packed up their belongings and left Cape Colony. They headed off into Africa to find a new place to settle. The journey was a long and difficult one. They eventually found a place to live and named their new territory 'Natal'.

Just four years later, the British invaded and took Natal also.

Once again the Boers went in search of a new homeland. This time they settled in two kingdoms, The Orange Free State and the Transvaal Republic. Now they called themselves 'Afrikaners', instead of Boers, to show that they were no longer Dutch settlers but Africans of European descent, who had a right to live there. Great Britain was too busy dealing with its other colonies to worry about the Boers settling in this dry and rocky area and so the British government decided to recognise these two new kingdoms as independent South African countries.

In their new homelands, the Afrikaners continued their way of life and enslaved the native population.

Tensions between the Boers and the British

Diamonds were found in 1871, along the banks of the Orange River between the two Boer colonies and the now British Cape Colony. No one had claimed this land, and so the British announced that it would now belong to the British Empire. An enormous mine called the 'Big Hole' was dug, and thousands of diamonds were extracted.

Miners in the Transvaal discovered gold in 1886. The Boers did not have the means to get all the gold out of the ground, so their government had to make a deal: British prospectors and businessmen could come and mine the gold, as long as the people of Transvaal got to keep part of it. The deposits turned out to be enormous, bringing huge wealth to the area.

The Governor of Cape colony in the 1890s, Cecil Rhodes, sent officials north of the Boer states to build another colony, 'Rhodesia'. British territory now surrounded the Boers, escalating tensions.

In 1899, Rhodes gave his officials permission to invade the Transvaal and claim it for the British Empire. Fearing the British would try and take the Orange Free State as well, the Afrikaners declared war on Great Britain.

The Boer War

Initially the war went badly for the British. Afrikaner soldiers took them by surprise in several towns but, after months of fighting, British reinforcements arrived and the tide of battle turned. Eventually, the Afrikaners began to surrender.

After the war had officially ended, gangs of Afrikaner guerrilla fighters continued to occupy certain areas and attack British soldiers and civilians. To break supply lines and stops these attacks, the British rounded up the civilians there and put them into camps. While these were called 'concentration camps', there was no intention to torture or murder. However, the residents were held in horrific and unsanitary conditions where disease killed thousands. The camps were badly overcrowded and provided insufficient shelter and food. Thousands more suffered malnutrition and starvation.

The Afrikaners and British finally signed the Peace of Vereeniging in 1902, uniting the warring colonies to form the Union of South Africa. However, the memory of these events would lead to years of bitterness and hatred between these new countrymen.

The Fashoda incident

In 1898, French colonies in Africa stretched from the Atlantic coast eastward, along the southern border of the Sahara, over an area covering modern day Senegal, Mali, Niger and Chad. Compared with other Europeans, the French treated the natives within their colonies well and often saw them as equals. They wanted to create a railway between the Niger River and the Nile, thereby controlling all trade to and from the region. They already had control over the caravan routes through the Sahara, and possessed an outpost near the mouth of the Red Sea.

Meanwhile, the British wanted to build a railway to link their lands in Southern Africa with their territories in East Africa (modern Kenya), and these two areas with the Nile basin, which was also under British control. The proposed route was often referred to as the 'red line' after Cecil Rhodes talked about painting the whole of Africa 'British red', when he spoke of colonisation.

If you draw a line from Cape Town to Cairo (the planned British route) and another from Dakar to French Somaliland (now Djibouti) by the Red Sea (the planned French route), they would cross in eastern Sudan, near the town of Fashoda (present-day Kodok). Both the French and the British needed control of Fashoda to complete their railways.

Tension was already high between these two countries. The French had for a long time hated the fact that Britain controlled Egypt and wanted to see them driven out. An outpost on the Upper Nile, which could serve as a base for French ships, would help them in this quest. Another idea they had was to build a massive dam in this area, cutting off the Nile's water supply and forcing the British out of Egypt. Both these plans had significant flaws and were unlikely ever to be carried out, but they still worried the British and created a great deal of tension.

Both countries sent out parties to take control of Fashoda. The French sent one hundred and twenty soldiers and seven officers from Brazzaville, led by Major Jean-Baptiste Marchand. They were to be met by two expeditions coming from the east across Ethiopia, one of which was led by Christian de Bonchamps. After an epic fourteen-month trek across the heart of Africa, the Marchand Expedition arrived on July 10th 1898. The de Bonchamps Expedition, however, failed to make it, after being ordered by the Ethiopians to halt, and then suffering accidents in the Baro Gorge.

On September 18th, British gunboats, led by Sir Herbert Kitchener, sailed down the river and arrived at the Fashoda fort. When the French and British met, both insisted on their right to Fashoda. News of the meeting was sent back to Paris and London, where both sides accused the other of aggression. Throughout September and October both nations began to prepare for war.

The British had a larger, stronger navy whereas the French fleet was badly built and poorly organised. The French army was far larger than the British one, but there was little it would have been able to do against Britain without efficient naval support. Faced with this disadvantage, the fact that it needed an alliance with Britain against Germany and the knowledge that many in Europe thought it stupid to waste lives and money on a remote part of Africa, France ordered its soldiers to withdraw.

Creating colonies

European nations were able to colonise areas of Africa in two main ways: by signing treaties and by using force. Some African leaders were willing to sign treaties either because they thought it beneficial to gain European allies or, in some cases, because they lacked a clear understanding of them or what their consequences would be. Where the native people put up more resistance, military force was used instead.

Once claims were made and borders were drawn, the Europeans had to come up with a plan for governing their newly acquired colonies. There were four main ways in which European nations ruled African colonies:

1 — *Company rule*

In the early days of colonialism, European nations allowed private companies to govern large territories in Africa. These companies were formed by businessmen who were interested in exploiting the natural resources of the land they were allowed to control. They had the power to set taxes and direct the natives in the area. The company concerned took responsibility for all of the expenses involved with running a colony, which represented a good deal for the mother country; it gained the political benefit of an additional presence in Africa without the cost.

The British East Africa Company was established in 1888 and colonized Kenya on behalf of Britain. It made treaties that claimed to offer protection to the various tribes of East Africa in exchange for them accepting its rule. The Company governed Kenya until 1893.

The British South Africa Company was formed in 1887. Under the control of Cecil Rhodes, it used force and coercion to colonize three territories in South-Central Africa: Nyasaland (Malawi), Northern Rhodesia (Zambia) and Southern Rhodesia (Zimbabwe). It governed these colonies until 1923.

These companies were eventually unsuccessful and failed to generate consistent profits. Governing a colony was expensive, and the companies faced opposition from Africans and missionaries over their harsh treatment of the native people. By 1924, all company rule had been replaced with some other form of government.

2 — *Direct rule*

The French, Belgians, Germans, and Portuguese used direct rule in governing their African colonies. They set up governments and created laws and regulations which the people there had to obey and follow. Under this scheme, the invading country tried to make Africans within the colony western — more 'civilised'. Native people were usually considered less important than Europeans.

European strategy was to 'divide and rule'; they implemented policies that intentionally weakened the natives' position and created situations which caused divisions between tribes.

Between 1444 and 1815, control of Senegal changed several times, passing between Portugal, France and Britain. The French had consistently held a trading post in the area since 1638 and ended the period as the colonial power.

Capt. Louis Faidherbe was governor from 1854 to 1865 (except for 1862). Within months of his appointment, he set about expanding the French held land towards inland territories, in particular the Niger region, hoping for control all the way across the continent to the Red Sea. He followed the 'Plan of 1854' which set out exactly how Faidherbe should proceed. Forts were to be created along the Senegal River, which ran East to West, with the aim of taking over the African acacia gum trade.

By 1860, Faidherbe's forts stretched inland as far as Saint-Louis, and he had put a stop to the taxes charged by local Moor tribes on goods transported up the river. He used a number of different tactics, including force and persuasion, to get control of the land he wanted, and sometimes acted beyond instructions from France. After the Battle of Logandème (18th May 1859), he ordered his men to burn the villages of the Fatick region to the ground. This followed no order from France.

Faidherbe had taken matters into his own hands.

He faced opposition from the local tribes, in particular from El Hadj Umar Tall, the Muslim ruler of the countries of the middle Niger. Umar Tall laid siege to the Medina Fort, in an attempt to drive the French out, but Faidherbe's men fought back, forcing both a Muslim retreat and the signing of a treaty over the land. He then set about westernising the territory with transport links, telegraph communication and fresh water supplies.

With Faidherbe in charge, the French empire was able to expand in West Africa. They treated their colonies as one large political and economic area. Local chiefs were replaced with French officials. Everyone in the territory became a citizen of France and was expected to follow French traditions.

French became the official language.

3 — Indirect rule

The British used indirect rule to govern their colonies. This gave power and responsibility to African rulers, who were then answerable to Britain. Lord Lugard, a colonial administrator, used this system first in Nigeria, and later brought it to British East Africa. It only really worked if the natives were organized in tribes with their own chiefs, which was not always the case. As a result, indirect rule could increase tensions between African groups, when power was given to selected individuals.

In 1912, Lord Frederick Lugard became governor of British-held land in Nigeria. At this time it was two separate areas, but Lugard's mission was to combine the territories into one colony. He received little opposition, except in Lagos. Once united, he set about trying to improve the colony by building hospitals, railways and harbours. He also claimed to be trying to both reduce alcohol consumption and suppress slavery. However, much of the funding for his projects came from taxes on imported alcohol and he permitted some slavery in northern Nigeria by wealthy families.

He failed to see native Africans as equals, entitled to an education, and did not seem to like Nigeria very much, spending half his time back in England.

The British controlled the army and taxation.

Almost everything else was left to co-operative natives.

4 — Settler rule

Sometimes huge numbers of European settlers came to live in a colony, intending to make the area their permanent home. In order for this to happen successfully, they needed political power and the ability to make money from the available resources. They needed to be more powerful than a native population which significantly outnumbered them. This was usually achieved through harsh and unfair treatment of the latter.

The 'White Man's Burden'

The British strongly believed that colonising Africa, and teaching its people British customs, was in Africa's best interests. They felt it was their duty to pass their knowledge and technology to the less fortunate and 'inferior' people of the Empire. Rudyard Kipling referred to this belief as 'The White Man's Burden', in his poem of the same name, but the British felt proud to carry this burden, and wanted to let those in the Empire know that they were willing to help them improve.

During colonisation large numbers of Christian missionaries arrived in Africa. Missionaries wanted to spread their message among the native people and end traditional customs they believed evil, convinced they were saving souls and enhancing lives. Sometimes their methods ran counter to the interests of the people they were trying to save. Missionaries often arrived separately, after colonisation, and spoke out against the treatment of the native people. However, most supported colonialism as it made it easier for them to propagate their religion.

Revision

What was the nature and impact of 19ᵗʰ century imperialism in Africa?

Why was there a scramble for colonies in Africa during the 19ᵗʰ century?

— Europeans felt that the larger their Empire, the more powerful they would become

— feelings of nationalism meant that each population wanted to see their country excel

— Africa held natural resources which could generate great wealth through trade

— the Berlin Conference provided a legitimate means of dividing up and claiming Africa

— Europeans saw it as their duty to spread their 'civilised' ways.

What different methods were used by Europeans to rule in Africa?

— company rule

— direct rule

— indirect rule

— settler rule.

How were Africans affected by European rule?

— rival tribes were sometimes forced to live together

— allied tribes were sometimes separated

— native Africans were often treated harshly by Europeans

— the native people were considered less important than white colonists and sometimes to be sub-human

— in some areas, natives were imprisoned, tortured, abused, mutilated and murdered

— slavery was abolished throughout most of Africa.

Did Europeans benefit from their colonies in Africa?

— money was made from the new resources

— the colonies were expensive to maintain

— disputes over territory caused hostilities between European countries

— Christianity was spread to new areas of the world.

Some questions for you to try

1   Why did explorers and missionaries travel to Africa in the 19th century?

2   Why was there a scramble for colonies in Africa in the late 19th century?

3   Was the Berlin Colonial Conference successful in its aim to stop European countries fighting?

4   How did France and Belgium treat people in their African colonies?

5   Was imperialism at all beneficial to Africa?

6   What does the phrase 'White Man's Burden' mean?

Chapter 7

The modernisation of Japan

At the beginning of the 19th century, the islands of Japan were ruled by a 'shogun' — a military general who inherited his position. Since 1600, that shogun had been from the Tokugawa family. Japan lived under a feudal system where feudal lords called 'daimyo' answered to the Shogun, and ruled domains called 'han'. The daimyo issued their own currency within their han and were protected by their 'samurai'. The samurai often lived a good life; some even had castles in which to live. Others were poorer and served their masters as officials rather than warriors. The daimyo and samurai controlled their land and the farmers and peasants who lived on it.

In the 17th century, the Tokugawa shoguns had been afraid that Christian missionaries coming into Japan would convert the Japanese to Christianity and destroy the traditional Buddhist faith. They were even more afraid that foreign armies would follow the missionaries and take over Japan. They became so worried that they decided that it would be best not only to keep all Christians out of Japan, but to keep *everyone* out of Japan. The Japanese felt that they had everything they needed and required nothing from the West. The shoguns passed a law forbidding Japanese people to travel to foreign lands and barred western merchants from docking in Japanese ports. An artificial island was created in one of Japan's harbours, Edo Bay, where only a few Dutch ships were allowed to land, just once per year.

For almost two hundred years, the Japanese cut themselves off from the western world. Despite these efforts, by the 19th century western ideas were finding their way to the Japanese people.

Many of them were beginning to wonder if such isolation was really a good idea.

Matthew Perry and the Black Ships

In August 1853, four 'black ships' arrived at Edo Bay and anchored offshore. Two were steam ships, which the Japanese had never seen before and thought were on fire. Commodore Matthew Perry was in charge. His task was to persuade the Japanese to open their ports and allow Americans to trade with them. They wanted to buy silks, ceramics and coal. Japan was full of coal and the Americans wanted it for their steam ships.

Perry told the Japanese that he had an important letter from the President of the United States and would only deliver it to a high official of the Emperor. Although Japan had an Emperor, he did not rule; the Shogun did. The Japanese decided to write a letter saying that a local governor called Toda was the Emperor's high official, and even signed it in the Emperor's name. When the Americans saw this fake letter, they were convinced and agreed to give Toda the President's one. This contained a threat: trade or risk being invaded!

The Japanese knew they could not win a fight against the Americans. They had only a few cannons and after years of peace, their samurai were no longer the fierce warriors they had once been. When Matthew Perry returned in 1854, they reluctantly signed the Treaty of Kanagawa, which forced them to open the ports of Shimoda and Hakodate to the United States, and to guarantee the safety of its sailors.

This was just the start for Japan. It was not long before European countries were arriving with their own trade treaties. Japan was closed no more.

Japan is open

Many Japanese were unhappy about these new treaties as Japan it seemed had little to gain. They called them the 'unequal treaties'. When a Japanese official signed another agreement in 1858, this time allowing Americans to live in Japan, a group of samurai attacked him and cut off his head as a punishment.

Soon foreigners were living all over Japan and having an effect on Japanese language, heritage and culture. And if that was not bad enough, they were refusing to follow Japan's rules. If a foreigner committed a crime, they were tried according to the laws of their own countries, not those of Japan. They also set their own taxes for importing and exporting goods; taxes which benefited them, not the Japanese.

The Shogun died in 1866, and twenty-nine-year-old Tokugawa Yoshinobu, took over. Yoshinobu could see that Japan was in trouble and he set about making changes to restore the country to its former glory. He tried to strengthen the army and promised his people that he would throw all foreigners out. But it was too little, too late. The people were fed up with the way the shoguns had been running Japan. The daimyo demanded that Yoshinobu resign and end the Tokugawa Shogunate for good.

Yoshinobu knew that more fighting in Japan would only make Japan weaker and provide an opportunity for America and other western countries to take advantage, so in 1868 he resigned.

He was marched off to his house under guard.

The Meiji Restoration

With the Shogun gone, some of the daimyo decided that the Emperor should be in put charge, who at this time was seventeen-year-old Mutsuhito. An Emperor had not ruled in Japan for nearly three hundred years, but the daimyo thought that this young one could be manipulated in their favour. Under imperial control, they hoped to renegotiate the unequal treaties and take control of the tariffs levied on goods coming into Japan.

The city of Edo, where the shoguns had ruled, was renamed Tokyo and became the imperial city. All lands that had belonged to the Shogun, his loyal daimyo or their samurai were now put under imperial control. The daimyo made the Emperor sign the 'statements of intent' in the Charter Oath, agreeing that there would be assemblies for open discussion ; that common people would be treated decently by officers ; and there would be no class restriction on employment.

Although many people thought these were good changes for Japan, many others who had lived well under the rule of the Shogun were very unhappy and it was not long before Japan was thrown into civil war. For a year, the Japanese who had been loyal to the Shogunate fought with the Japanese who were loyal to the Emperor. Finally the Emperor's army overpowered and destroyed the Shoganate one using guns they had bought from the West.

This time in Japan became known as the Meiji Restoration because the rule of the Emperor had been restored. ('Meiji' means 'enlightened one'.)

Western ideas in Japan

Although the Emperor was back in charge of Japan, the daimyo who put him there were very powerful. They wanted to learn the ways of the West and embarked on an ambitious program of social, economic and constitutional reform to transform Japan from a feudal agricultural state into a modern industrial society. They knew this was the only way that they could compete with the rest of the world. If they remained as they were, it would only be a matter of time before someone else invaded. Japan needed to stand as an equal power in order to preserve its integrity and traditions.

The Japanese made a deliberate effort to learn as much as possible about the West and sent representative to Europe and the United States to learn about their societies.

Foreign powers could see that Japan had changed and were keen to share their knowledge. The French taught the Japanese about building and repairing ships ; the Americans showed them how to mine coal ; and the British helped them build factories and taught their workers to spin.

Japan's Ministry of Industry put all these new skills into action and financed coal mines, shipyards and textile mills. New factories were opened, also with public funds. As its expenditure rose in the 1870s and 1880s, the government sold off most of their factories to private investors. This resulted in individual families gaining wealth and control over the economy. Industrial zones grew enormously and huge numbers of people moved to the areas where jobs were being created. The number of agricultural workers decreased, but new methods of farming, better types of crop and effective use of fertilizers meant that production increased. National railways were constructed and communication systems developed.

Many western ideas were adopted by Japan including the style of clothing. Initially it was just the wealthy who wore items such as the bustle or suit but, by 1872, the Japanese people were told that they were no longer to wear Japanese robes but western clothing instead.

Western technology was adopted all over Japan, as was the western calendar. Gas lighting was introduced into the cities as early as 1872 and was followed by electricity in Tokyo in 1887.

Schools were built, with education compulsory for four-year-olds introduced in 1872. Traditional Japanese skills were taught alongside western learning. Universities were founded from 1877 reducing the number of students sent abroad to study.

A new system of defence was created to strengthen Japan. British warships were introduced into the Japanese navy and officers were trained by the Royal Navy. A new army was created, modelled on the French and German systems, replacing the Samurai. Soldiers were paid a salary rather than receive land, as the Samurai had. Conscription was introduced in 1873 and every man had to join up on turning twenty-one. He would then remain in the army for four years and then serve three more as a reservist. Soon the Japanese army was efficient, equipped with modern arms, and well organised.

In 1876 the samurai were told they could no longer carry swords in public. Giving up their sword meant their whole way of life was changing, and they were not happy. Previously, the carrying of arms was what distinguished them from the ordinary people and made them special. Things and changed ; the samurai, who had once lived in castles and protected their daimyo, were no longer needed.

The Satsuma Rebellion

The majority of samurai were content despite having their status abolished. Being better educated than most of the population, they easily found employment, becoming teachers, gun makers, government officials, or military officers. But some, particularly those from the Satsuma domain, were not prepared to relinquish their title so easily. Led by Saigo Takamori, they gathered a samurai army and prepared to fight the newly conscripted one.

The Samurai Satsuma army had their swords, and traditional armour, but their imperial enemy had modern western weapons. For eight months the two sides fought, but inevitably the samurai were eventually overpowered and destroyed.

A new constitution

In Japan's new form of government the wealthy daimyo held a lot of power. Initially, any criticism of this government was censored and suppressed but, as time went on, more and more Japanese people called for a change. Advisers were sent all over the world to study different systems and decide which best suited Japan's needs. Eventually a new Japanese western-style constitution was written. The Emperor would be head of state, with overall supreme power, but he would choose his prime minister and cabinet from a small group of distinguished leaders. The cabinet would then make the policies. Two assemblies of representatives would be elected to pass laws for Japan, just as in western society.

The Sino-Japanese War

West of Japan lay the little country of Korea. After many years of trading with just China, Korea signed a treaty with Japan and began trading there also. China and Japan decided to make a deal. As neither country wanted the other to take control of Korea, they agreed that it would be protected by both, and that neither could send soldiers there without the agreement of the other.

In 1894 a Korean religious group started to collect weapons and plan a rebellion. These poverty-stricken peasants were miserable with their lives and angry with their leaders. King Kojong of Korea sent a message to China asking for Chinese soldiers to help defeat the rebels. The Qing emperor agreed, borrowed a British warship, loaded it with soldiers and sent them towards Korea. When the Japanese found out that China was sending soldiers without their permission they were very suspicious. They believed the Chinese were out to capture Korea for themselves and attacked and sank the ship.

The Chinese were furious and declared war. However, this war was fought neither in China nor Japan, but in Korea.

China's army turned out to be no match for the Japanese soldiers, armed with western weapons. In less than eight months, the Japanese had marched from southern Korea up into China, and the Chinese had to sign a peace treaty that gave Korea total independence from China, and also ceded considerable territory to the Japanese.

The Sino-Japanese War alerted the rest of the world to the new strength of Japan. By using western ideas and western technology, Japan had very quickly become an industrial competitor with an extremely strong army. Britain made an alliance with Japan in 1902, as a useful ally in the Pacific. This treaty gave Japan prestige and security and would lead to further alliance during the First World War.

Conflict with Russia

During the 19th century, Japan's neighbour, Russia, had built a new railway in the land it acquired from China. The Trans-Siberian Railway ran from Harbin, a large city in the northern province of Manchuria, all the way down to Port Arthur on the Yellow Sea, providing Russia with easy access to the Pacific Ocean and the rest of the world. Russia had convinced China to lease Port Arthur to them for twenty-five years, in exchange for a large sum of money.

Having already crept into China, Russia decided that it now wanted Korea too. The Japanese were not at all happy about this idea as they had plans to take Korea for themselves. They also disliked the idea of Russia having influence over territory which was so close to them.

Japan sent ambassadors to Moscow with a message for Tsar Nicholas II, asking him to remove Russian soldiers from Port Arthur and Manchuria. Nicholas refused. The ambassadors were called home and told to take no more messages to the Tsar. Breaking off diplomatic relations in this way was usually an indication that war was imminent. Nicholas II was not worried; for centuries Japan had been an old-fashioned, isolated country without a modern army. In contrast, Russia had the third largest navy in the world — only France and Great Britain had more ships. The new army of Japan had not existed for very long. Russian officers were so sure the Japanese would not dare attack the Russian ships and soldiers in Port Arthur that they did not even warn them. This was a terrible mistake.

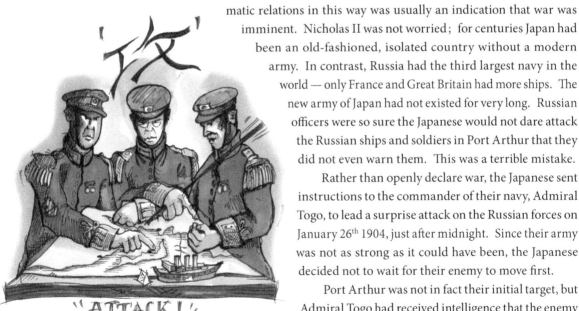

Rather than openly declare war, the Japanese sent instructions to the commander of their navy, Admiral Togo, to lead a surprise attack on the Russian forces on January 26th 1904, just after midnight. Since their army was not as strong as it could have been, the Japanese decided not to wait for their enemy to move first.

Port Arthur was not in fact their initial target, but Admiral Togo had received intelligence that the enemy ships there were on alert and ready to intercept. Togo therefore decided to aim his attack directly at Port Arthur instead. His intelligence had been incorrect ; the Russians expected nothing.

When they got near enough, the Japanese fired sixteen torpedoes at the Russian battleships. Only three ships were hit, but two were the most valuable in the fleet. Onshore, the Russians were so surprised that they initially thought the battleships were just carrying out target practice.

This attack on Port Arthur was just the first. Admiral Togo launched attack after attack on the larger Russian force, destroying many ships, including the *Petropavlovsk*, the flagship of the Russian navy. The Admiral of the Russian navy sank with it. For almost five months, Japanese ships kept Port Arthur under siege until finally, the Russian forces had to surrender.

With the Russian navy defeated, the Japanese marched against the Russian soldiers on land. They fought ferociously and, at the Battle of Mukden, the Tsar's army was defeated. The war was over, and Japan had won. This was also the first time a European army had been defeated by an Asian one.

It was clear to the whole world that Japan was now the master of the East, not China.

The President of the United States, Theodore Roosevelt, helped to arrange a peace treaty between the two countries. Russia was forced to surrender territory, including Port Arthur, and Japan gained control over Korea. Roosevelt was awarded the Nobel Peace Prize for his involvement.

The 19th century had seen Japan move from total isolation to become a dominant world power.

Revision

How effectively had Japan modernised itself by 1914?

What was the impact of Perry's mission to Japan?

- — Japan was forced to trade with America

- — the Treaty of Kanagawa was signed

- — other countries followed America's example and forced trade agreements on Japan

- — foreigners started living in Japan

- — many Japanese became discontented with the way their country was being run.

Why did the Meiji Restoration occur?

— the Shogun had not prevented an American invasion and lost the support of many

— the Shogun resigned to prevent civil war

— the seventeen-year-old Emperor was placed in charge but was a puppet of the daimyo.

How westernised was Japan by 1914?

— the Japanese had learned shipbuilding, coal mining and factory production from Europeans

— railways had been built, improving transport and communication

— traditional Japanese robes were banned and western clothing adopted instead

— the samurai had lost their status and a new army created, with national service

— Japan had adopted a western-style constitution and government, with the Emperor as the head of two assemblies.

Was Japan a great power by 1914?

— advances in shipbuilding, weaponry and military training had significantly strengthened Japan

— the Japanese military defeated both the Chinese and the Russians proving themselves to be a world power.

Some questions for you to try

1 What role did the daimyo and samurai play in early 19th century Japan?

2 How significant was Perry's mission in modernising Japan?

3 What effect did the Treaty of Kanagawa have on Japan?

4 Why did the Meiji Restoration occur?

5 Was the removal of the feudal system responsible for the modernisation of Japan?

6   Were social, industrial or economic changes more important in the modernisation of Japan?

7   How was Japan's military changed?

8   Was the Anglo-Japanese Alliance of 1902 important for Japan?

9   Was Japan fully modernised by 1914?

Chapter 8

The path to global war

8.1 Preconditions

Alliance

Between 1873 and 1914, a number of alliances were forged by the countries of Europe. An alliance is an agreement made between two or more countries that they help each other in times of conflict. They were important for security, but they also meant that a country had no option but to declare war when an ally did so.

After the Franco-Prussian War, Chancellor Bismarck wanted to prevent the German government from getting involved in any more hostilities, so he actively sought alliance with neighbouring countries. Germany, Russia and Austria-Hungary formed 'The League of the Three Emperors' (Dreikaiserbund) in 1873, which would inhibit France from declaring war again. By 1879, Russian influence was spreading and Russia claimed land in the Balkans. Nervous of its expansion, Germany signed the 'Dual Alliance' with Austria-Hungary. Each country promised to protect the other should Russia invade.

In 1881, Austria-Hungary made an alliance with Serbia, promising to protect Serbia from Russian invasion. Italy joined the Dual Alliance between Austria-Hungary and Germany in 1882, making it the '*Triple* Alliance'.

Wilhelm II became the new Kaiser in Germany in 1888. Bismarck had many disagreements with him and was forced to resign in 1890. Under Bismarck, German relations with Russia and Austria-Hungary were friendly, but Wilhelm II did not see the value of any such alliance. He upset Russia, ending the League of Three Emperors.

Russia decided to join forces with France instead, creating their own alliance in 1892. They promised that if either country was attacked by Germany, they would both declare war in response.

With all these agreements being made, Britain began to look around for allies. British politicians thought about an alliance with Germany against France and Russia. However, German policy under the Kaiser was so badly managed that Britain felt forced to look to France and Russia instead. She established friendly relations with France in 1904 and Russia in 1907. They formed the 'Triple Entente', agreeing to work together against Germany if necessary.

Arms race

The years between 1871 and 1914 saw the Germany Empire going from strength to strength. Industrial revolution had increased Germany's production and by the turn of the century the output of German factories had overtaken even that of British ones. Many German people felt that, like Britain, their country should have a worldwide empire. Kaiser Wilhelm II thought a new, more aggressive approach would be the key. In 1900, the German government ordered the building of a huge new navy to rival that of Britain.

The British had a policy, called the 'Two Power Standard', that the Royal Navy always had to be as big as the next two strongest navies in Europe put together. They intended never to be outgunned at sea, and so responded to the German shipbuilding with a new type of powerful battleship called the *Dreadnought* in 1906. The Germans then began building similar ships of their own.

Nervous about the growing fleet of German ships, the British ordered the building of even more substantial battleships, called 'super dreadnoughts', in 1911. These were no longer slow coal-fired ships, which required large numbers of the crew manning the engines: they were fuelled with oil. However, Britain had no oil and would therefore need to bring it in from abroad. Persia had large deposits so, for a while, Britain and Russia argued about who should have control there. Russia finally won but, because of a deal between the Persian Shah and an Englishman named D'Arcy in 1909, the British got access to all the oil they wanted.

The Anglo-Persian oil company concerned later became British Petroleum (BP).

During this time, France had been building up its army and Russia had been building railways, ready to carry their troops into Europe. Germany then set about expanding its army to outnumber the French.

Tension in Europe was growing.

8.2 Provocation

The Moroccan crisis

For years European countries had been competing for land and had almost totally divided up Africa between them. Morocco was an as yet uncolonised African country which France wanted to add to its empire. Germany objected. On March 31st 1905, Kaiser Wilhelm II visited Tangiers, made a speech favouring Morocco's independence and demanded an international conference on its future; the Algeciras Conference was held in 1906 and thirteen nations came to help settle the dispute. Austria-Hungary supported Germany, but Britain, Russia, Italy, Spain, and the United States all supported the French taking control of Morocco's police and banks.

For a while tension seemed to be relieved but, just five years later, another crisis arrived. This became known as the Second Moroccan (or Agadir) Crisis. It started when France sent troops to Fez to fight Moroccan rebels, who objected to French involvement. The Germans accused the French of trying to take complete control, and sent their warship *Panther* to Agadir, hoping to force them to give up the 'French Congo'. The British were suspicious of the German presence and thought they must be planning to build a naval base. They had a naval base nearby at Gibraltar and did not like having German ships so close. They too sent warships to Agadir, forcing Germany to back down.

Once again a meeting was held and another agreement was signed in November 1911. Germany would accept French rule in Morocco in return for territory in the French equatorial African colony of Middle Congo (now the Republic of the Congo). War had been avoided, but the fact that the British had backed France twice against Germany caused a deep rift between these two countries.

Trouble in the Balkans

Before 1878, much of the Balkan Peninsula fell within the Turkish Ottoman Empire. Macedonia, Albania, Serbia, Bosnia, Bulgaria and Romania all belonged to the Turks. The tiny country of Montenegro had managed to remain independent and Croatia belonged to Austria–Hungary.

Towards the end of the 19th century, the Turks and the Russians fought a war which caused the Ottoman Empire to lose a lot of territory on the Balkan Peninsula. The

129

Russians had declared war against the Ottomans over their treatment of Chistians in Bulgaria. When it was over, the Ottoman Empire had to cede Romania and most of Asia Minor (Anatolia) to Russia, and agree to give Bulgaria its freedom. This arrangement made the rest of Europe nervous. It made Russia much larger and more powerful, and turned Bulgaria into a strong and loyal ally.

Great Britain, France, Germany and Austria combined to intervene, insisting that Asia Minor be returned to the Ottoman Turks. They also decided that, since it would always fight on Russia's side in any war, Bulgaria would have to become smaller. The Bulgarians were forced to return the southern part of their territory to the Turks. Russia was able to retain influence over the north as it was to be ruled by the Tsar's nephew by marriage, Prince Alexander of Battenberg. The Bulgarians in the south were furious. They wanted to be free to join the north, not to be part of the Ottoman Empire again. The northern and southern parts of Bulgaria opted to reunite. Alexander supported the Bulgarian people, but this put him in a difficult position and he upset his uncle and other European leaders by not consulting them. He also upset the Bulgarian people, when he tried to compromise with their leaders, and was forced to abdicate in 1886. Now that Bulgaria was no longer tied to Russia, the rest of Europe was no longer worried and it was allowed to remain united.

In 1878, Europe decided that control of Bosnia would be taken from the Turks and handed over to Austria-Hungary. In 1903, after several uprisings, Serbia also obtained freedom from the Turks and became an independent country. The Serbians felt that Bosnia should also be free from outside rule and form part of Serbia. They were so intent on this idea that they threatened Austria-Hungary with war. With the alliance between Serbia and Austria-Hungary now broken, Russia mobilised its forces to protect Serbia. Germany, allied to Austria-Hungary, mobilised as well and prepared to threaten Russia. This became known as the 'Bosnian Crisis of 1908'.

War was avoided when Russia, and then Serbia, backed down.

Macedonia also tried to break free from the Ottoman Empire In 1903. Rebels joined together in the city of Krusevo and declared themselves independent of Turkish rule. This became known as the 'St. Elijah's Day Uprising'. Sultan Abdulhamid ordered his soldiers to march into Macedonia and kill the rebels. The violence disgusted many Turkish people, who began to turn against their Sultan. A revolutionary group formed called the 'Young Turks', which wanted freedom from Imperial rule. They were supported not only by the Turkish people but also by the Christian countries of Europe, and made plans to take over the Empire. They convinced the Ottoman army to join them in demanding that the Sultan bring back the Turkish parliament, which he had disbanded. Faced with a popular rebellion that had support within Europe and even among his own soldiers, Abdulhamid abdicated and fled.

In 1909, the Young Turks, now in power, announced that they would do what the people wanted. All Ottomans over twenty would be allowed to vote and Christians would be treated equally, although it would still be a predominantly Muslim country. This meant that they too faced conscription into the army. Islamic laws were replaced with secular ones, which were not based on any religion.

The Young Turks decided that everyone within the Empire would speak Turkish and be loyal to the same government. They sent messengers to other European countries, asking for advice about how to make Turkish farms and factories more modern and productive.

Macedonia and Albania, still part of the Empire, did not want these changes; they wanted freedom. The Young Turks were encouraging more Muslims to move into these areas and the Christians living there were suspicious of the new government's motives. The Balkan countries decided they would fight for the independence of Albania and Macedonia. The forces of Serbia, Bulgaria, Greece and Montenegro joined together, with the help of the Russian government, and marched against the Turks. So began the First Balkan War, in 1912. The Ottoman army did not stand a chance against these combined forces and surrendered.

Albania was given its freedom, but the situation with Macedonia was more complicated.

Serbia, Bulgaria, and Greece started to argue with each other about how they would divide up Macedonia, and so began the Second Balkan War, in 1913. Feeling betrayed, Bulgaria turned against its allies. It's campaign was, however, unsuccessful and Macedonia was divided up with Bulgaria receiving a much smaller portion than Serbia and Greece. Now all the Balkan countries were free from Ottoman rule, but they harboured a deep-seated hostility.

Feeling vulnerable, Bulgaria made an alliance with Austria–Hungary. Still angry at being attacked, Serbia became more and more hostile towards Bulgaria. Serbia was also angry with Austria-Hungary, which still controlled the small Balkan state of Bosnia, believing that it too should be set free.

Tensions between these countries were very high.

The Shooting

On June 28th 1914, a group of six Serbian teenagers, calling themselves 'The Black Hand', decided to show how much Serbia hated Bulgaria and Austria by killing the heir to the Austrian throne, the Archduke Franz Ferdinand. The plan was to throw a bomb into the Archduke's car as he made an official visit to the Bosnian city of Sarajevo, but the boy given the job missed. The explosion went off behind the car instead, seriously injuring two members of the Archduke's party. Immediately, police charged into the crowd and grabbed the culprit. He tried to swallow a capsule of cyanide to kill himself but could not get it into his mouth properly. He was arrested at once and dragged off to jail.

Seeing that the plan had failed, the five other boys fled. One of them, nineteen-

131

year-old Gavrilo Princip, went into a coffee shop nearby to calm himself down. When he finished his coffee and left, he saw the Archduke's car passing again, heading to the hospital to visit the victims of the bombing. Princip acted quickly; he drew his gun and shot into the car. He swallowed his cyanide capsule as he was quickly overpowered and arrested, but the capsules the gang used were out of date and just made them sick. The car sped away, but it was too late. The Archduke had been shot in the neck and his wife in the stomach. Both died before they reached the hospital.

Austria insisted that the assassination must have been planned by the Serbian government. They denied the allegation but, on July 28th 1914, the Austro-Hungarian Empire declared war on Serbia. For a third time, the Balkan countries were at war; but this was to be no 'Third Balkan War'.

It would become the First World War.

8.3 Outbreak

When Austria-Hungary declared war on Serbia, two other countries were immediately involved: Russia, a Serbian ally, began to gather its forces to attack Austria and sent troops to its borders with Germany and Austria-Hungary; Germany, an ally of Austria, declared war on Russia.

Two days later, Germany also declared war on France.

The Germans knew that France would ultimately join hostilities because of its alliance with Russia. Instead of waiting for an assault, the German government launched their 'Schlieffen Plan' (devised before 1905 by army chief-of-staff, Alfred von Schlieffen). They had anticipated the outbreak of war and thought themselves well prepared.

They knew they would be at a disadvantage, being situated between their two main enemies. Their plan was to attack and defeat France first, then turn and fight the Russia army, which they expected to take a long time to mobilise. They believed Russia would need around six weeks to prepare for war, giving them time to deal with France first.

The plan was to march into France, capture Paris and force the French to surrender. In 1870, it had taken just ten weeks for Prussia to defeat France, so the Germans did not expect it to be that difficult.

They believed France would attack along the border it shared with Germany (the Alsace-Lorraine frontier). This was a mountainous area, well-fortified by the French, making it difficult for the German army to attack. If the Germans could cross further north, they could get behind the French and trap them. While the main German army moved north and entered France through Belgium, Italy, which was part of the Triple Alliance and therefore duty bound to support Germany, would be responsible for defending the Alsace-Lorraine frontier.

After capturing Paris, the German army would use the well-developed railway system to travel from France back to the east frontier of Germany ready to face the advancing Russian army.

Belgium had previously, in 1839, declared its neutrality, and the other powers of Europe had signed a treaty promising not to invade it. The Germans knew that the Belgian army was badly equipped, poorly trained and unprepared, so they expected little opposition when their troops marched through.

One slight problem was Britain, which had promised it would support Belgium in the event of an invasion. However, the Germans felt confident that British help would never arrive, or if it did, that it would be too late anyway.

As far as the Germans were concerned, this was going to be a quick and easy war.

Revision

What caused the First World War?

Did the alliance system make war more or less likely?

— alliances made countries feel stronger and deterred their enemies from attacking them

— alliances created tensions between countries

— alliances gave some countries no option but to join in the conflict

— alliances meant that everyone was waiting for war

1879 : Dual Alliance : Germany and Austria-Hungary become allies against Russia

1881 : Austria-Hungary promises to protect Serbia from Russia

1882 : Italy joins the Dual Alliance, creating the Triple Alliance

1890 : Bismarck's Dreikaiserbund (League of three Emperors) abolished, leaving Russia feeling annoyed and vulnerable

1892 : Russia allies with France instead

1904 : Britain and France become allies

1907 : Britain and Russia become allies and, with France, form the Triple Entente.

How far did colonial problems create tensions between the great powers?

— European countries had been competing with each other for years

— tensions already existed

— Moroccan Crisis : Germany felt that it was treated unfairly and that the other countries of Europe were siding against her.

Why were problems in the Balkans difficult for the great powers to resolve?

— Russia was getting too powerful, so France, Germany, Britain and Austria intervened

— Balkan territories wanted freedom and objected to foreign interference

— Austria took Bosnia; Serbia objected; the Bosnian crisis of 1908 ensued

— people of different religion disagreed over rule

— different races wanted independence from each other.

How did the assassination of Franz Ferdinand lead to war?

— tensions between Austria, Bosnia and Serbia were already very high

— a Serbian shot Franz Ferdinand, the heir to the Austrian throne

— Austria-Hungary declared war on Serbia

— Russia declared war on Austria, in support of Serbia

— alliances forced other countries to join in

— Germany declared war on Russia and then France.

Some questions for you to try

1 Was the alliance system responsible for the tension between the great powers?

2 Were the Balkans Wars or the assassination of Franz Ferdinand more responsible for the start of World War I?

3 How far was the arms race responsible for the conflict?

4 Why did the crisis over Morocco in 1911 increase tensions in Europe?

5 Did the assassination of the Archduke Ferdinand make war inevitable?

6 Did Germany cause the conflict to become a World War?

Chapter 9

The First World War (1914-18)

9.1 The first year of war

The Schlieffen plan, did not quite work as Germany expected. The German Kaiser, Wilhelm II, asked the Belgians to let his army march through their territory so he could attack France, but they refused. This was the first blow to his well-thought-out idea, but it failed to deter the Kaiser, who felt he had no choice but to simply invade Belgium too. The invasion began on 3rd August 1914.

The following day, Germany received an ultimatum: withdraw by midnight, or Britain would declare war. Even though the Germans knew this was a possibility, they had not expected Britain to stand by its promise to defend Belgium. Britain had strong royal connections with Germany, but it feared her becoming too powerful. When the German army failed to withdraw, Britain had the excuse it needed and declared war.

The Belgians put up more of a fight than the Germans were expecting. They delayed the German advance as long as they could, but their capital city of Brussels fell on the 20th August. The British moved quickly. Within a week, the British Expeditionary Force (BEF) of 125,000 men had arrived in France to support the French army. The British and French had been aware of the Schlieffen Plan since 1913 and were well prepared. France had developed 'Plan 17': an invasion of Germany via the Alsace-Lorraine frontier, followed by an attack on its capital city of Berlin, while the Germans were busy trying to get through Belgium.

Not only did passing through Belgium take much longer than the Germans had planned, but the Russians also mobilised faster than expected. They exploited the delay, and invaded Germany, crossing its eastern border on 17th August. The French had time to put Plan 17 into action and were attempting their invasion as well, through Alsace-Lorraine. The German commander, Count Helmuth von Moltke, had to split his army and defend Germany on more than one front after all.

On 23rd August, as the Germans had almost passed through Belgium, they were met by the BEF, commanded by Sir John French, at the Belgian town of Mons. The Germans were surprised; they had not expected to see British soldiers yet. The comparatively small British force held the German army back long enough to allow the French valuable time to retreat and reorganise.

Plan 17 had meanwhile failed. The French army had been unable to invade Germany, despite the lack of Italian support, for which the Germans had hoped. French soldiers in brightly coloured red and blue uniforms had marched against German machine gun fire and been massacred. Three hundred thousand French soldiers had been killed. Many were officers, easily identified by their white gloves. Those who survived regrouped with the retreating French army near the Marne River.

The Germans had planned to head straight to Paris, but with so many men now deployed on other fronts they lacked the power. They were forced instead to head south and face the regrouped French army. The Battle of the Marne lasted four days. The French commander, General Joffre, even brought additional troops from Paris, using various forms of transport, including six hundred taxis. The exhausted Germans were forced to retreat to the Aisne River, and dig trenches to defend themselves. These began as small pits, in which a single soldier could hide, but they proved of such value that they were soon extended. The Allied Forces followed their example and dug down too.

The British Army needed more men. A massive campaign was mounted to encourage more to join the army. Recruiting posters made people feel they had a duty to do so; men who did not were often shamed by others. 'The Order of the White Feather' encouraged women to give out white feathers — a sign of cowardice — to men who had not volunteered. Women from the 'Mother's Union' put great pressure on women to encourage their husbands and sons to volunteer. Government propaganda gave people a rosy picture of the war and exaggerated the cruelty of the enemy. Censorship denied them the real news from the front. By September 1914 there were half a million volunteers. Another half a million had joined by February 1915.

Both sides knew how important sea access was and now pushed north, extending their trenches, in what became known as 'The Race for the Sea'. The Germans captured Ostend and Antwerp; the Allies held Dunkirk and Calais, and, after a brief struggle, took back Ypres.

By the end of 1914, the trench lines stretched 470km — all the way from the Belgian coast down to Switzerland. The two armies had reached stalemate. Trenches were easy to defend, but hard to attack; new tactics would be needed for the war to progress.

Stalemate on the Western Front

The trenches were about ten feet deep and heavily fortified. They were dug in a zigzag formation to make them harder to attack, and to help protect occupants should the enemy make it across 'no-man's land' (the area of land between the opposing forces) or an explosion take place. Behind the front line, communication trenches allowed troops to move forward and back. They were supposed to be replaced every eight days, but in reality it was more like every two or three weeks. 'Saps' (short dead end trenches) were dug out into no-man's land to allow listening posts to be set up. The sides of the trenches were supported with wood, corrugated iron and sandbags. Machine guns and lines of barbed wire defended them. Sentries were positioned every few yards to spot an enemy attack, particularly at dawn and dusk, when low light made it more difficult to see anyone approach.

The generals in charge were not used to this kind of fighting; they knew more about the type of battle that took place on a big field, where cavalry charged in, followed by foot soldiers, all backed up by artillery. They were faced with something new, which required strategic planning and creative tactics. To break through the enemy's barbed wire, they tried using artillery. It was not very successful, and warned the other side that an attack was coming. Soldiers then had to climb out of their trenches and try to run across no-man's land, which was often thick with mud. Shell craters, filled with water, blocked their path. Dead bodies littered the area, sinking into the mire. The attackers would fall under heavy fire from machine gun and cannon. Once across, they had to break through what was left of the barbed wire, climb into the enemy's trench and 'take' it, armed only with rifle and bayonet.

Life in the trenches

Life in the trenches was very harsh. As well at the constant bombardment from the enemy, the trenches were full of rats, lice, fleas and mud so thick that men sometimes drowned in it. The ground was continuously churned up, making it difficult to deliver supplies. Thousands of soldiers suffered 'trench foot' when they could not keep their feet dry. They became infected after being wet and muddy for weeks on end; some developed gangrene and had to have their feet amputated. On top of this, temperatures dropped during the winter months, causing many to suffer frostbite.

The trenches were unhygienic. The lack of flushing toilets, together with decaying dead bodies and horse manure, left a horrendous smell. Creosote was sprayed as a disinfectant, but the constant state of filth invited rats and increased the risk of disease.

An ordinary soldier was paid one shilling a day and survived mostly on rations of bully beef, jam and tea. Each day began before dawn with a 'stand to', as this was the most likely time for the enemy to attack. The rest of the day was spent taking turns on sentry duty, collecting food rations and supplies from the support trenches, collecting water in old petrol cans, repairing and digging trenches, and filling sand bags. At dusk, after another 'stand to', they could rest. Activity began again after dark as men were sent out to spy on the enemy to collect information, repair barbed wire and rescue wounded comrades from no-man's land.

When they were not on the frontline, troops waited in reserve a few miles away. This time was spent training, mending roads, polishing boots and buttons, looking after the horses and visiting local towns and villages. Sporting matches were arranged and professional entertainers booked to put on shows for these 'resting' troops.

Nobody was used to trench warfare. Neither side could break the stalemate; new tactics had to be found. One was the use of poison gas. The Germans used it against Allied troops for the first time at Ypres, in 1915. A yellow mist came drifting across no-man's land, causing the men to run for their lives. Those lying injured in no-man's land could be heard coughing in pain as they inhaled.

Three different types of gas were used during the following years of the war: chlorine, which left victims drowning on water produced in their lungs; phosgene, which caused the lungs to froth in yellow gunk; and 'mustard gas', which burned the skin and lungs.

Initially, the Allies had no protection. Instead, soldiers were advised to place a sock or handkerchief, soaked in urine, over the nose and mouth. Eventually, proper gas masks were issued. Victims had to endure after effects; many suffered lung disease in later life. The Allied governments condemned the German use of gas, but it was not long before they used it too.

9.2 Verdun and the Somme

In February 1916, the Germans attacked the French fortress of Verdun. A massive artillery barrage was followed by advancing infantry, using gas shells and flame throwers. Huge losses were suffered by both sides, and the French were forced to retreat.

The French commander, Philippe Petain, dealt harshly with his soldiers and ordered them to retake the lost ground. Any who refused were threatened with execution, but he also provided his men with plenty of supplies, and brought in reinforcements. The battle went on for months. By November, the French were beginning to win.

In order to help the French, the British ordered a counter-attack at the Somme, further up the line, to the north-west. The aim was to make the Germans fight two major battles at once, forcing them to divide their forces.

The British took months to prepare. Huge stores of ammunition had been built up. Captured enemy trenches were examined to see how they were built. Despite it being discovered that the Germans were using concrete to protect their dugouts, the plan went ahead unchanged.

For six days prior to the attack, the British tried to clear the German barbed wire with a massive artillery barrage. This failed miserably, but the British Commander, Sir Douglas Haig, ordered an advance regardless. On 1st July 1916, British soldiers were sent 'over the top' with orders to advance slowly in a line towards the German trenches. Their slow progress made them an easy target and gave the Germans time to get ready for the attack. As if the British were not vulnerable enough already, a previously unexploded mine was detonated, covering them in debris. Those who made it as far as the German trenches used hand grenades to clear them.

Although some success was seen, most gains were lost once more by the evening.

Fifty-seven thousand Britons were killed or wounded on the first day alone.

The battle dragged on till November, with the British advancing around fifteen kilometres in some places. By the time it ended, more than a million soldiers had been killed, of whom more than four hundred thousand were British.

The Germans were not beaten at the Somme, but they took a severe battering and the battle probably helped to wear them down.

Douglas Haig — the man behind the decision to send the soldiers 'over the top' — was branded a hero, promoted to Field Marshal and made an Earl, but some have since blamed him for the huge number of casualties and given him a less flattering title. 'Butcher of the Somme'.

Tanks were used for the first time during the Battle of the Somme. Haig took the decision to send in the forty-nine he had available rather than wait for the arrival of more, feeling that surprise was more important than number. Tracks on their wheels allowed tanks to pass over very rough ground and over barbed wire with no problem. Ordinary gun fire could not stop them. It had no effect on their heavily armoured body.

They should have allowed the British army to break the deadlock, but it took a while to develop effective tactics and overcome difficulties. Early tanks often broke down, got stuck in the mud or toppled over into a crater. Their crews faced intolerable noise, suffocating fumes and overwhelming heat.

Captured tanks were sometimes repainted and used by the Central Forces against the Allies.

Soon the Germans were developing and using their own.

9.3 Tipping the balance

Tanks and planes

Tanks were not really used effectively until The Battle of Cambrai in November 1917, but as the war progressed they became more and more important.

The military use of aeroplanes also began during the First World War. Not surprisingly, they made a massive difference to the way wars were fought. To begin with, they could survey the battlefield and bomb enemy positions. Both sides used planes and balloons to look for weak points along the trenches where it would be better to attack. Early aircraft were slow and difficult to fly. Arming them with an ordinary machine-gun was a failure as it was hard to aim, and there was a danger of damaging your own machine, especially the propeller.

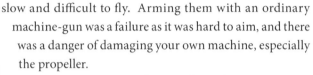

By 1915, new synchronised machine-guns were being used which could shoot safely between the spinning propeller blades. Now, one man could both fly the plane and fire the gun at the same time; before they had always needed two people. Fighters were used to escort bombers on raids, and to attack enemy planes in spectacular air battles.

German pilots fought in groups which patrolled the skies twice a day. The most famous of these was the one led by Baron Manfred von Richthofen, also known as The Red Baron.

The German army also introduced hydrogen-filled airships called 'Zeppelins' to carry bombs. In May 1915 they used these to mount a major raid on London. Zeppelins were easy to shoot down though, because they were so big.

Both sides developed planes which could be used for long-distance bombing raids. The first serious raid on Britain was in May 1917 when ninety-five people were killed in Folkestone. Britain sent bombers into Germany too, with devastating effects on its citizens. This really changed the dynamics of the war. It was no longer the kind where soldiers left to fight, while their families stayed safely at home. Now, everyone was at risk, everywhere.

The developments made during the war left a lasting legacy. Bombers had become able to travel hundreds of kilometres without refuelling. The new technology would later be used to set up the first passenger airlines. The Royal Air Force was formed in 1918 out of the army's Royal Flying Corps and the navy's Air Service. By the end of the war, the RAF had more than *twenty thousand* planes.

Away from the Western Front

The First World War did not stop at the Western front. The Royal Navy's blockades in the North Sea and the Baltic were very important in wearing Germany down.

The British patrolled the North Sea and the Baltic Sea with the aim of stopping food and supplies reaching Germany, either directly or via neutral countries like the Netherlands and Scandinavia.

Naval blockades also prevented German ships from getting out into open sea where they could attack Allied vessels. German warships initially attacked the British coastline, though with little effect.

Despite all the shipbuilding prior to the war, the British and German dreadnoughts only fought one battle. The Battle of Jutland took place in May 1916 in the North Sea, when each fleet tried to trap the other. Neither side won, although both claimed victory. The British felt they had won because the German fleet returned to port and never again ventured out. The Germans felt they had won as they had escaped and returned safely to port.

The only effective weapon the Germans had against the Royal Navy was the 'U-boat' — a submarine. Initially, they were careful not to attack ships from neutral countries or any passenger vessel. Britain realised this and started shipping arms and ammunition in the holds of liners.

On 7th May 1915, German U-boats torpedoed the British ocean liner *The Lusitania*, without warning. The ship exploded and sank. Twelve hundred people died, mostly civilians.

The rest of the world was furious. *The Lusitania* was not carrying soldiers; it was a passenger ship, filled with civilians. This broke the rules of war; German submarines could torpedo British warships, but they were supposed to leave civilian vessels alone. The Germans claimed that the ship was carrying weapons, which has since been the topic of much controversy. Some people have suggested that the boat exploded so easily because of the ammunition on board. Others have gone as far as suggesting that the British encouraged the attack by leaking information about its secret cargo.

The United States government was particularly angry because more than a hundred of the drowned passengers were American citizens. For the first time, Americans began to think that perhaps the USA should get involved in the Great War. To prevent America joining in, the Germans agreed to abide by 'the cruiser rules' and give warning before they attacked, though they did not always stick to this.

By 1915, other countries were joining in. Italy entered the war, but not on the side everyone expected; they joined the Allies (Britain, France and Russia). Britain had won over the Italians with an offer of land surrounding the Adriatic Sea. Also on the Allied side were Australia and New Zealand, who had sent troops, known as the ANZACs.[1] Turkey had joined the Central Powers (Germany) and was busy preventing Allied troops from passing and supporting the Russian army on the Eastern Front.

Winston Churchill, the First Lord of the British Admiralty, planned the Gallipoli Campaign, both to support the Russians and ultimately to defeat the Central Powers. The idea was to attack Turkey's Gallipoli peninsula, defeat the Turkish army and continue past Constantinople (Istanbul) into the Black Sea and the shores of Russia. It was a disaster from start to finish. To begin with, inexperienced British soldiers and ANZACs were sent, with battle-hardened troops remaining on the Western Front.

The assault began with twenty-three Allied warships attacking the Dardanelles straits in April 1915. They were met with heavy gunfire and many mines. When three ships sank, Admiral Robeck prematurely called off the attack, not knowing that the Turks had almost run out of ammunition.

A second attack was launched on the tip of the peninsula. British soldiers, again inexperienced, were sent from Egypt to support the ANZAC troops. A supply ship was to follow, but suffered problems and had to return to Egypt to be reloaded. This delayed the assault by a month, during which the Turkish army discovered the Allies' plan and prepared well. General Sir Ian Hamilton was put in charge of the Allied attack. He had little experience and maps almost a decade out of date.

The attack was launched on 25th April 1915. British troops landed on the beaches and awaited further orders. ANZAC troops arrived in boats nearby, but strong currents blew them off course and they landed further away than planned. The allies and Turks both dug trenches and made unsuccessful attempts to gain ground. Huge losses were suffered on both sides. Allied supplies were unable to land and soldiers soon ran short of ammunition and replacement guns.

Hamilton requested more troops and an experienced commander. He was sent more inexperienced soldiers and General Stopford, who had never before seen wartime action. Stopford's troops arrived in Suvla Bay on 6th August 1915. It was dark when they landed and they struggled to locate each other. For two days they sat on the beach awaiting supplies and orders. The water tankers sent to supply the troops with fresh water had not been loaded with hoses and could not get the water to the shore. The men became weakened by dehydration and the Turks gained time to prepare defences.

In November 1915, with the weather getting colder and the men suffering frostbite, the Gallipoli Campaign was called off. Hundreds of thousands of men had died, with nothing gained. Neither Hamilton nor Stopford saw action again. Churchill resigned. This was not to be his last experience of war, however: he later became the British Prime Minister during WWII.

---

[1] Australia and New Zealand Army Corps.

On the Eastern Front, the Russian army had mobilised quickly and the British newspapers talked confidently about the 'Russian steamroller' crushing the opposition as it advanced into Germany. It was not to be. The Russians did catch the Germans off guard though, getting ready in less than two weeks with six million men. The Germans were forced to send troops east before they had defeated France, and so the Schlieffen plan failed. But the Russian advance was also a failure. Their plans were made in haste; they were not prepared for a long campaign and needed to advance quickly. Their army was poorly organised, with many officers inexperienced and too few weapons. Many soldiers had to wait for someone to get killed before they could get hold of a rifle.

The Russians were faced with both Germans and Austro-Hungarians, and had a border to defend that stretched eight hundred miles. A stalemate soon developed on the Eastern Front, like the one in the west. In 1915, Tsar Nicholas II took personal charge of the Russian army. This was a big mistake as he was soon blamed for its failure. The war effort put a great strain on Russia; civilians went hungry so that troops could eat. With their Tsar on the front lines, leaving the running of the country to his wife, the Russian people soon began to question his leadership.

The Russians did make one successful attack on the Central Powers, when in June 1916 General Alexei Brusilov ordered a massive Russian advance. In the first three weeks the Russians made great progress, but by December they had been driven right back, losing many men.

Demoralised soldiers began to desert the army.

Faced with huge losses, food shortages and an absent leader, revolution broke out in Russia in February 1917. Tsar Nicholas II was forced to abdicate and a new Provisional Government took over. It continued the war effort without success.

In August 1917, the Commander of the Russian army, General Kornilov, turned his men away from the front lines and aimed them at the government instead. In desperation, the government asked an opposition group, the communist Bolsheviks, for help against Kornilov's army. Led by Vladimir Lenin, they stepped in with their own Red Army and stopped Kornilov, but the Provisional Government had proved itself a failure.

In a second revolution in October 1917, Lenin and the Bolsheviks took power and set about withdrawing from the war. On 3rd March 1918 they signed the Treaty of Brest-Litovsk, losing much treasure and vast areas of important land to the Germans, but Russia was officially out of the war.

War on the home front

The First World War was a war unlike any previous one. Not only were soldiers lost from countries all over the world, but civilians were affected too. Despite government propaganda, ordinary people in Britain could see that the war was not the great heroic ideal they had imagined, and they took responsibility for sending much needed supplies to the front line.

On 8th August 1914, Britain passed the Defence of the Realm Act (DORA), which censored news-papers and banned discussion of the war in public. It also banned invisible ink in overseas mail; the ringing of church bells, unless Britain was invaded; and the sale of binoculars. Factories were taken over for war production; British summertime was introduced to increase daylight working hours; pub opening hours were reduced and alcohol regulations enforced; and voluntary rationing began.

Casualties seemed to be mounting, both home and away, yet the war dragged on without suc-cess. Large numbers of soldiers were coming home crippled or blinded, and fewer men were joining up. So many men were being killed and wounded on the Western Front that there were not enough volunteers to replace them. There was also a growing feeling in Britain that it was unfair that some could refuse their military duty. In the winter of 1916, when it seemed the war might never end, Great Britain passed a new and frightening law. Conscription, also known as the 'draft', was introduced. The government could now order young men to join the army and fight, whether they wanted to or not. All single men aged between eighteen and forty-one were called up. When it became clear there were still not enough recruits, married men had to join up too.

People who did not believe in fighting were called 'conscientious objectors'. They were treated as criminals and sent to prison; some were even shot. They were seen as traitors.

Many of the original volunteers came from heavy industries like coal mining. There arose a shortage of workers in these industries; without them Britain could not supply the army. After conscription began there were even fewer men available to do the vital jobs, so women started taking their places in the pits and factories.

By 1917 food was running short and the government took over land to create allotments. Vegetables were grown in public places and more space was allocated to farming. Thousands of women joined the Women's Land Army and helped on the farms. The British Prime Minister, David Lloyd George, commanded the navy to protect merchant ships from U-boat attacks.

Despite all these efforts, full scale rationing was ordered in 1918. Everyone got coupons which they had to hand over when they bought beer, butter, sugar or milk. When the week's coupons ran out they could buy no more until the following week. Some people hoarded food, partly because they were afraid it would run out, and partly because of increasing prices. They would sell it on later creating a black market. There were shortages of some things but no-one starved. Most people ate as much as they did before the war. However, this was new territory and the government had never before been this involved in organising people's daily life.

As the war continued, women played an increasingly important role in many areas as more and more went out to work, on top of running the home and caring for family. Without women stepping into these roles the country would literally have ground to a halt. Delivering coal, farming, factory work, teaching, policing and operating buses and trams, all became typical women's work.

Women also played an important role away from home. They went to the front to work as nurses and doctors; joined the Women's Army Auxiliary Corps, working as cooks, typists, storekeepers, carpenters and drivers; and worked as telephonists in France.

Women who had previously been 'in service' to wealthy families now left to contribute to the war effort. This drastically altered the face of Britain, as life for both the rich and poor changed for ever. Now people of all classes would work and socialise alongside each other.

Prior to the First World war, the suffragist and suffragette movements had been fighting for equal rights for women. Suddenly, women's lives had changed dramatically and war gave everyone a common focus. Demonstrations and campaigns were put on hold. Women had finally been recognised as having the same capability as men. In fact, they had become so important in work that unions started to worry that men would not get their jobs back when the war finished. Prime Minister Lloyd George promised that men would both return to their job and receive a higher wage than women.

Although women had not quite achieved equal rights, equal recognition or equal pay, their lives were changed forever by the war. It had become acceptable for them to do lots of different jobs. In 1918, those over the age of thirty, who owned property, were rewarded with suffrage (allowed to vote).

Armistice

In 1917, Germany came up with a new idea to win the war. The Germans sent a coded telegram to the German Ambassador in Mexico, telling him to make a deal with the Mexican government. If Mexico would fight on the German side then, on winning the war, they would help Mexico retake the land lost in their war with America. That land included New Mexico, Texas, Utah, Nevada, Arizona, California and part of Colorado.

Before the Germans could actually make this deal however, British cryptographers managed to get a copy of the telegram and decode it. American newspapers published the content, so that citizens all across the country could read it. Under growing pressure, the United States declared war with Germany on April 6th 1917. The US president, Thomas Woodrow Wilson, had previously felt that his country should stay neutral in the Great War but, following the sinking of the Lusitania and now this direct threat, he changed his mind. He now believed that the United States had a duty to fight against

Germany and help save Europe from dictatorship. He announced that America had to join the war so that 'the world may be made safe for democracy'.

American soldiers were deployed to Britain and France. Just as in Great Britain, women rushed to help on the home front by doing the jobs that men left behind when they joined up.

The arrival of American forces finally tipped the balance in the war against the Central Powers.

On 21st March 1918 the Germans launched one final offensive. Operation Michael was aimed at the Somme, which was at this point the weakest part of the Allied front line. The Germans had not attacked this area in two years and the Allies were caught off guard. In the early hours of the morning, through thick fog, the Allied trenches were hit with machine gun fire, explosives, flamethrowers and gas. Highly trained German 'Stormtroopers' were able to push back the British line. Over the next few weeks the Germans advanced, gaining confidence they could at last win the war. They even came within thirty-five miles of Paris and bombarded the city with their gigantic 'Kaiser Gun'.

Their success was not to last. Germany could not provide their troops with enough weapons and supplies to keep the advance going. Many German soldiers left the front line to loot French towns.

The Allies fought back hard against the exhausted German army with fresh reinforcements from America and were eventually able to regain lost ground.

With exhausted soldiers, low morale, a major flu epidemic breaking out, food shortages and crumbling allies, Kaiser Wilhelm II put Prince Max von Baden in charge of the German government on 3rd October 1918. Just as in Russia, the new government failed to make immediate changes. Strikes and protests broke out in Germany.

On 29th October, German sailors mutinied at Kiel, refusing to fight on. Communist supporters seized power in Munich on 6th November. Kaiser Wilhelm II abdicated on 9th November, fleeing with his family and a carriage load of treasure to the Netherlands. On the same day, Prince Max von Baden handed power over to Friedrich Ebert and Germany became a republic.

Trench warfare had worn the Germans down. Mutinies, food shortages and revolution made it impossible for them to carry on. The new government agreed an armistice with the Allies on November 11th 1918. All over the world, exhausted soldiers heard the news at 11am and celebrated.

Although peace had finally arrived, as many as ten million soldiers and ten million civilians had died. In France, Great Britain and Germany, almost every family had lost a brother, husband or father to the Great War. It was over, but every country in Europe had suffered. Among the Allies, Great Britain had lost nearly a million men. Another million and a half had been wounded — hundreds of thousands so badly that they would never again enjoy a normal life. France suffered even more: almost a million and a half French soldiers had been killed, with millions more wounded. Russia had lost nearly two million, and Italy over half a million. Among the Central Powers, nearly two million German, over a million Austrian and half a million Turkish and Bulgarian soldiers lost their lives.

The war had also wrecked so much. Houses and factories were in ruins, roads and railways had been blown up and coal mines destroyed.

Revision

How was the Schlieffen Plan intended to work?

— Germany would attack and defeat France by passing through Belgium, then turn its army around to fight against Russia

— Germany would not have to fight on two fronts at the same time.

How was the invasion of Belgium important?

— Britain gained the excuse it needed to declare war on Germany

— Belgium put up greater resistance than expected, which delayed the German advance, allowing time for Britain to deploy forces and Russia to prepare its defences.

How effective was the British Expeditionary Force (BEF)?

— Germany had not expected it, giving the BEF the advantage of surprise

— although driven back, it provided France with much needed support

— its involvement prevented Germany from capturing Paris, and ultimately France.

Why did both sides introduce trenches?

— trenches were a successful defence against newly developed weapons

— they offered soldiers protection from bullet and shell.

Why did the war become bogged down in the trenches?

— trenches were easy to defend but difficult to attack

— new tactics took time to develop for a kind of war that was entirely new.

What was living and fighting in the trenches like?

> — soldiers had to face mud, rats, lice, trench foot and a shortage of supplies
>
> — they slept in 'dug outs', though the Germans used concrete bunkers
>
> — they were on duty for long periods of time
>
> — they were sent 'over the top' and had to cross 'no-man's land' to attack the enemy
>
> — resting troops trained and were entertained by performers.

How important were new developments such as tanks, machine guns, aircraft and gas?

> — defence against new weapons required the development of new tactics and equipment
>
> — they became more successful towards the end of the war
>
> — the use of aeroplanes paved the way for a dedicated air force and passenger flight.

What was the significance of the battles of Verdun and the Somme?

> — Germany was forced to divide its forces and fight in two places at the same time
>
> — there was massive loss of life due to Haig's tactics (on the Somme)
>
> — tanks were used for the first time.

Who won the war at sea?

> — the British navy successfully prevented German supply ships from reaching port and reduced the number of German attacks on allied ships
>
> — both sides claimed victory at the Battle of Jutland
>
> — German U-boats sank the Lusitania.

Why did the Gallipoli campaign of 1915 fail?

> — both commanders and troops were inexperienced
>
> — forces were withdrawn prematurely from the Dardanelles Straits
>
> — ships were delayed or not properly equipped to deliver supplies
>
> — soldiers were not given clear instructions.

Why did Russia leave the war in 1918?

— Tsar Nicholas II had been forced to abdicate

— General Kornilov led his troops against the provisional government

— there was a shortage of food

— Russia had suffered huge losses

— a Bolshevik (communist) revolution was under way.

What was the impact of war on civilian populations?

— food became short in supply and rationed

— homes were destroyed

— bombing raids caused terror and death

— most families experienced loss

— men were forced to join up, through conscription

— women began to work, in a wide variety of jobs, for the first time.

What was the importance of America's entry into the war?

— fresh troops helped turn the war in favour of the Allies

— America could prevent another war with Mexico.

Why was the German offensive of 1918 unsuccessful?

— German soldiers were so short of supplies, they were forced to loot local villages

— exhausted German soldiers faced fresh American ones

— flu and other sickness prevented many Germans from fighting.

— the German army lost support from people back home.

Why did revolution break out in Germany in October 1918?

— people were fed up with war

— the new government did not make changes quickly enough

— there was a naval mutiny at Kiel

— support grew for communism

— the Kaiser abdicated.

Why did Germany sign an armistice?

  — a new government had taken over

  — German soldiers were exhausted

  — revolution had taken attention and support away from the war

  — there was a shortage of food

  — people did not want to see any more men die.

Some questions for you to try

1 How important to the failure of the Schlieffen Plan was Belgium's reaction to invasion?

2 How important were technological innovations on the Western Front in changing warfare?

3 How significant was the Battle of the Somme to Britain?

4 How important was the contribution of women to the British war effort?

5 How significant to the course of the war was Russia's defeat by late 1917?

6. How significant in ending the war was the outbreak of revolution in Germany in October 1918?

Chapter 10

A century of turmoil and progress

The 19th century saw huge changes take place worldwide. It was a time of cruelty, brutality and greed, yet also a time of discovery, invention and improvement. To some extent, this era saw human nature at its worst. People with money and power thought themselves elevated, and treated those who they felt to be unequal as second-rate citizens. Slavery, child labour and the repression of women were all considered perfectly acceptable. People endured terrible conditions, but learned from it and made changes to benefit the future.

Britain changed from a farming society to one of industrial strength. Life for its people reached a miserable low, before seeing improvements in working conditions, living conditions, wages, health care and schools. These 19th century decisions became the foundation for the creation of systems still in use today. The British Empire spread round the globe and held a degree of power not seen before or since. The British dominated trade, repressed native peoples and spread their religion in the belief they were helping and benefitting those less fortunate. Their interference did help bring an end to abominations like slavery, funeral sacrifice and foot binding.

After purchasing French lands in the Louisiana Purchase and winning Mexican territory through war, America had become huge, but the states failed to see eye to eye on the running of their union. Civil war turned Americans against each other and saw almost a whole generation of men killed. It saw slavery finally abolished throughout the union, yet equality between races remained a long way off; some might argue, it still has not been reached.

France had seen Kings and Emperors fail to meet the needs of the people and cause conflict with neighbouring countries. Through several uprisings, the French learned that ordinary people had strength in numbers and the power to change their future if they stood together. French attempts to improve life triggered revolutionary ideas across Europe.

Germany and Italy both became new countries, formed from the desire for unity, strength, and power among the ordinary people. They may not have become free from monarchy, as many desired, but their countries were now independent. Both peoples held strong nationalist ideas and would soon be makings plans towards world domination.

Africa, India and China saw the new industrial strength of European countries threaten, invade and oppress their people. The 'invaders' thought native customs far inferior to their own, and set about the removal of these 'heretical' cultural traditions. In the eyes of many African, Chinese and Indian people, the white man became a symbol of evil and created scars that would take generations to heal.

Japan was forced to join the rest of the world, learned its enemies' strengths and used them to elevate itself and become a world power. Soon it would threaten its neighbours; America, in particular, would live to regret disturbing this sleeping lion.

People all over the world learned that strength and power lay in the masses and not in their former Kings and Emperors. The ordinary man learned that he had the power to shape his future and fought for the right to vote and have his say. Women were still denied that privilege. They would have to fight for their rights in the *next* century.

Huge developments in technology changed the way many people lived. They also gave industrialized countries an enormous advantage over the rest of the world, which continues to this day.

The 19th century saw violence, hunger and repression, but we live the lives we do today thanks to those people who campaigned for a better system.

Time line

18th century — industrial revolution in Britain; political revolution in France

1701   Jethro Tull invents the seed drill

1709   Abraham Darby discovers how to make coke

1712   Thomas Newcomen invents the first really successful steam engine

1714   George I becomes King of Great Britain and Ireland

1727   George II becomes King of Great Britain and Ireland

1730   Townshend improves farming through crop rotation

1733   John Kay invents the Flying Shuttle

1756   British attacked in Calcutta

1760   George III becomes King of Great Britain and Ireland
       large scale enclosure begins

154

1761   Bridgewater Canal built

1765   James Hargreaves invests the Spinning Jenny

1768   Arkwright's Spinning Frame in use

1771   Cromford Mill opens

1775   Britain goes to war with its American colonies

1779   Samuel Crompton invents the Spinning Mule

1781   James Watt uses steam to turn a wheel

1783   America gains independence

1784   Henry Cort invents new method of making wrought iron

1785   Edmund Cartwright invents the Power Loom

1789   French Revolution

1792   London Corresponding Society is formed

1793   Napoleonic War begins
       Eli Witney invents the Cotton Gin (USA)
       George Macartney arrives in China

1795   Treasonable Practices Act passed

1796   Edward Jenner discovers SmallPox vaccine

1799   Corresponding Societies Act passed

19th century — civil war in America; unification within Europe; imperialism elsewhere

1802   Health and Morals of Apprentices Act passed (Britain)

1804   Richard Trevithick builds a steam locomotive (Britain)

1806   Napoleon defeats Prussia

1807   slave trade abolished (Britain)

1811   Prince George becomes Regent (Britain)
       Luddite Riots

1815   Napoleonic War ends
       Vienna Congress held, giving rise to the Concert of Europe

1819   Robert Owen's Factory Act passed (Britain)
       Peterloo Massacre
       Zollverein established in Prussia

1820   George IV becomes King of Great Britain
       Louisiana Purchase and Missouri Compromise (USA)

1820   British take Cape Colony from Boers in South Africa

1824   Combination Act repealed (Britain)

1825   Stockton to Darlington railway opens
       Amending Combinations Act passed (Britain)
       Hungarian become the official language of Hungary

1827   Slavery banned in northern states (USA)
       Lord William Bentinck becomes Governor of Bengal

1830   William IV becomes King of Great Britain
       Manchester to Liverpool railway opens
       Three Glorious Days riots; Louis Phillipe becomes the Citizen King of France

1831   Italian secret societies rebel against Austrian rule
       Nat Turner revolt (USA)

1832   Sadler Report written (Britain)
       Reform Act passed
       Six Acts passed (Austria)

1833   Althorp's Factory Act passed (Britain)
       British Government starts awarding grants to schools

1834   Poor Law Amendment Act passed (Britain)
       Tolpuddle Martyrs transported
       Grand Consolidated Trade Union formed

1836   London Working Men's Association formed

1837   Victoria becomes Queen of Great Britain

1838   Robert Stephenson completes the London to Birmingham railway line
       People's Charter proposed (Britain)

1839   First Opium war begins (China)

1840   British railways adopt London Time
       Frederick William IV becomes King of Prussia

1842   The Mines Report is written (Britain)
       Mines and Collieries Act passed
       Edwin Chadwicks' report on sanitary conditions

1843   First Opium War ends; Treaty of Nanjing signed (China)

1844   Graham's Factory Act passed (Britain)

1844   The Railway Act passed (Britain)

1844   Ragged Schools established (Britain)
        Rochdale Society open first co-operative store

1847   Fielden's Factory Act passed (Britain)
        Otto von Bismarck elected to Prussian Assembly

1848   Public Health Act is passed (Britain)
        economic depression and famine in Europe
        revolt in Sicily (January)
        Louis Phillipe driven out of France (February)
        riots in the German states
        National Workshops established (France)
        Five Days of Milan (March)
        Vorparlament set up in Frankfurt
        April/March Laws established in Hungary
        National Workshops closed; June Days Uprising (France)
        riots and unrest in Hungary
        Louis Napoleon elected in France (December)
        James Broun-Ramsay, Marquess of Dalhousie, made Governor-General of India

1849   Russians aid Franz Joseph in suppressing Hungarian riots
        Frederick William rejects Frankfurt Parliament's offer of German crown
        Sicily brought back under control
        Victor Emanuel II becomes King of Piedmont-Sardinia
        Prussian Union planned

1850   Erfurt Union formed (Germany)
        Frankfurt Diet formed
        Compromise of 1850 (USA)

1852   Louis Napoleon declares himself Emperor of France
        Camillo de Cavour becomes first Prime Minister of Piedmont-Sardinia

1853   Crimean war begins (between Britain and Russia)
        Matthew Perry and the Black Ships arrive in Japan

1854   Treaty of Kanagawa signed (Japan)

1856   Crimean War ends
        Henry Bessemer invents the Bessemer Process (Britain)
        Garibaldi's soldiers arrive in Naples (Italy)

1856   Second Opium War begins (China)

1857   Sepoy mutiny (India)

1857   Dred Scott Decision (USA)

1858   Wilhelm I becomes Regent in Prussia
       Treaty of Tientsin signed (China)
       Government of India Act passed (Britain)

1859   Piedmont and France declare war on Austria
       Harper's Ferry rebellion in Virginia (USA)
       British envoys arrive in Beijing

1860   Abraham Lincoln is elected President (USA)
       Garibaldi hands over power to Victor Emanuel (Italian states)
       Second Opium War ends (China)

1861   American Civil War begins
       Italy unified; Victor Emanuel becomes King
       self-strengthening movement begins (China)

1862   Emancipation Proclamation, Abraham Lincoln (USA)

1863   Schleswig-Holstein problem (Germany)
       Reconstruction Plan, Abraham Lincoln (USA)

1864   Louis Pasteur discovers microbes (France)

1865   American Civil War ends
       Abraham Lincoln assassinated; Andrew Johnson becomes US President
       13th Amendment to US Constitution
       Ku Klux Klan formed

1868   14th Amendment to US Constitution
       Meiji Restoration begins (Japan)

1869   Ulysses S. Grant elected President (USA)

1870   Forster's Education Act passed (Britain)
       Franco-Prussian War
       Naturalization Act passed; 15th Amendment to Constitution (USA)

1871   Germany unified; Wilhelm becomes Emperor

1872   Chinese school boys sent to study in USA

1873   League of the Three Emperors created (Russia, Austria-Hungary and Germany)
       Joseph Chamberlain becomes Mayor of Birmingham

1877   Satsuma Rebellion (Japan)

1878   Factory and Workshops Act passed (Britain)

1878   Austia-Hungary takes control of Bosnia

1879   German and Austria-Hungary form the Dual Alliance

1880   Standard Time adopted in Great Britain
schooling becomes compulsory in Britain
scramble for Africa begins

1881   Austria-Hungary promises to protect Serbia from Russia

1882   Italy joins the Dual Alliance, creating the Triple Alliance

1884   Berlin Conference held to decide the future of Africa

1888   London Match girl strike

Wilhelm II becomes Kaiser in Germany

1889   London Dock Workers strike

1890   Bismarck resigns ; Wilhelm II ends the League of Three Emperors

1891   schooling becomes free in Britain

1892   Russia and France form an alliance

1894   Sino-Japanese War in Korea

1898   Fashoda Incident (Africa)

1899   Boxer Rebellion (China)
war breaks out again between the British and the Boers (Africa)

20ᵗʰ century — alliances and the First World War

1902   Peace of Vereeniging signed (Africa)
Britain and Japan form an alliance

1903   Serbia becomes an independent country and threatens Austria-Hungary with war

1904   Japanese attack Port Arthur
Entente Cordiale — alliance between Britain and France

1905   First Moroccan crisis

1906   Algeciras Conference

1907   Triple Entente created between Britain, France and Russia

1908   Bosnian Crisis

1911	Sichuan Rebellion (China)
	Second Moroccan crisis
1912	Chinese emperor abdicates
	First Balkan War
1913	Second Balkan War

1914	June	28th	Archduke Franz Ferdinand assassinated
			World War I begins
	Aug.	3rd	Germany invades Belgium
		4th	Britain declares war on Germany
		17th	Russia invades Germany
		20th	The Germans finally defeat Belgium.
		23rd	The Germans and the BEF meet at Mons
	Sep.	5th	Battle of the Marne
	Oct.	8th	Germans capture Ostend
		15th	Germans capture Antwerp
		18th	British and French recapture Ypres from the Germans.
1915	April	22nd	Battle of Ypres
		25th	Gallipoli Campaign
1916	Feb.	21st	Attack on Verdun begins
	May	31st	The Battle of Jutland
	June	4th	The Brusilov Offensive
	July	1st	Battle of the Somme begins
	Sep.	15th	Tanks used for the first time
1917	April	6th	America declares war on Germany
	May	25th	First German air strikes in Folkestone
1918	March	3rd	The Treaty of Brest-Litovsk
		21st	Operation Michael launched
	Oct.	3rd	Prince Max von Baden heads the German government
		29th	Revolution breaks out in Germany
	Nov.	9th	Kaiser Wilhelm II abdicates

Appendix

Answering examination questions

When answering exam questions, look at the number of marks the question is worth. This will give you a good idea of how much to write.

'Describe' questions

For 'describe' questions, write in full sentences and include as many relevant points as you can remember, in the order in which events occurred. You will get one mark for each relevant point and an additional mark for supporting detail. So for 4-mark questions you either need to put four different points or two points, each with explanation or illustration.

For example:

Describe the Sicilian revolution of 1848-49. (4 marks)

The Sicilian revolution was the first Italian revolt in 1848. It began in Palermo and was a revolt against Bourbon rule in Sicily. The people wanted to return to the constitution of 1812 which had been abolished in 1815. The rebellion spread all across Sicily with only Messina remaining loyal to the King. The Bourbon army didn't manage to retake control of the island until May 1949.

'Why?' questions

For 'why' questions you need to give reasons why the event happened. Try to give all the reasons. Usually, there will be both short- and long-term factors involved. Long-term factors are those that have been brewing for a long time; short-term factors are those which give the final push. For 6-mark questions, you will need to make two or three relevant points and explain each one, giving details.

For example:

Why was there a revolution in Hungary in 1848? (6 marks)

Hungary was part of the Austro-Hungarian Empire and had been ruled by the Austrian Emperor Ferdinand since the 1815 Concert of Europe. In the years leading up to 1848, the Hungarian people were becoming increasingly dissatisfied with their situation and started to talk about independence from Austria. However, the country was filled with people with many different ethnic backgrounds who all wanted their culture and history to be recognised and to be free from Austrian rule.

As the dissatisfaction grew, Klemens von Metternich, the Austrian chancellor, tried to end this type of talk, by tightening censorship and reducing freedom of the press. When news of events in France reached the Austro-Hungarian Empire, Metternich panicked and prematurely fled. This encouraged revolutionaries to act.

The Hungarian revolution was led by Louis Kossuth, a Hungarian of Magyar descent. He was an excellent public speaker and soon had a large following. He demanded independence and reform in Hungary, wanting the people to have a greater say in the running of the country, particularly those who were also Magyar.

'How far?' questions

For 'how far' questions, you need to discuss the topic. You need to discuss all the ways in which you both agree and disagree, giving evidence. You might be asked how far you believe a certain aim has been achieved. Discuss what has been achieved, and also what hasn't yet been achieved. Sum up you discussion with a conclusion, which will usually involve you giving your own opinion. Your opinion won't be judged right or wrong; you get marks for explaining and illustrating it.

For example:

'During 1848, revolution was more successful in France than in other European countries.'

How far do you agree with this statement? Explain your answer. (10 marks)

In 1848 revolution broke out in France, Hungary, the German states and the Italian states.

In France, Louis Philippe, the Citizen King, was removed, finally ending the monarchy, and a new republic under Louis Napoleon began, seeing reforms that benefitted the people. Sadly, a lack of understanding of the new political system and their options, led the French people to choose a president, who would in 1851, become a new, power hungry Emperor and dictator. There were far better candidates, but the people didn't really seem to understand their options.

The other European revolutions of 1848 failed to achieve lasting change and the original rulers remained in power. However, unlike France, these other countries were neither united nor independent, and faced the disadvantage of interference by other states.

Although they didn't succeed in their aims, the revolutions did have some degree of success. In the Italian states the people had seen the power they had when they stood together and new freedoms were granted, especially in Piedmont-Sardinia. Hungary had a taste of independence and in Prussia Frederick William IV had been forced to bend to the will of the people on several occasions.

To conclude, I agree with the statement that France was more successful than the other European countries as it saw the greatest changes in 1848, but also feel that the other revolutions shouldn't be seen as failures as they all achieved some degree of success which would set them on a path for future independence.

'Source/evidence' questions

When answering questions based on source and evidence, ask yourself:

— When was it written/created?

— Who wrote/created it?

— Why was it written/created?

— How useful is it?

Knowing the answers to these questions will help you evaluate how useful the evidence is and understand why it may or may not agree with other given source evidence.

When was it written/created?

First decide whether the source is primary or secondary evidence. You can do this by looking at the date, which is usually written in italics underneath.

Primary sources were written around the time of the event; secondary sources were written some time afterwards. If it was created at the time, the creator will have lived through the events depicted, which gives the evidence a greater degree of accuracy. However, personal experience will also lead to personal opinions, so the evidence is likely to reflect this and be biased. Bias is not bad, and does not make the source useless — far from it. Personal opinion gives us a real insight into how some people thought and felt at the time, but bias does need to be taken into consideration.

Secondary sources are created after the event and so lack that personal touch. However, creators were able to look at the event from various angles and so these sources are usually less biased and give a more general view of the event.

Who wrote/created it?

Look at the information underneath the source to see who produced the evidence. If it is one of the figures you are familiar with then think about their likely viewpoint of the event. If they would have held strong views one way or another this needs to be taken into consideration.

Why was it written/created?

Consider why the source was created in the first place. Was it written as a private message for just a select audience, or was it created to influence a large public audience. With this information you can consider whether you feel the evidence is reliable and trustworthy, or a piece of propaganda designed to provoke a particular response.

How useful is it?

Finally consider how useful the evidence is. All sources can be useful to some extent, even biased propaganda. It all helps to build a picture of the way different people thought and felt.

Essay questions

Writing essays can seem rather daunting as they require a lot more words! But it's really just an opportunity to discuss the topic further and look at it from different angles. However, marks can easily be accumulated by understanding how essays are put together.

Introduction

This should state what the essay is going to be about. It should refer to the question and comment on how there is more than one view/opinion/side to take into consideration and a brief outline of what these opposing views might be.

For example:

How important to the failure of the Schlieffen Plan was Belgium's reaction to invasion?

Germany had put together the Schlieffen Plan many years before the start of World War I, and believed that it would easily lead them to victory. The plan however was a failure. One major factor was Belgium's response to its invasion. However, this was not the only reason for its failure. Britain, Russia and Italy also made moves that Germany was not expecting.

This essay will look at those moves and discuss just how important Belgium's reaction was in the plan's failure.

Main body

This is where you will discuss the different viewpoints, opinions and key facts, allocating a different paragraph to each one. State clearly what the viewpoint or fact is in your opening sentence of each paragraph. Make clear points backed up by examples and link each back to the essay title. Linking back is very important as it shows the examiner that you are carefully considering the question asked and not just waffling. You don't need to put in everything you know about the topic, just the bits that are relevant to the essay title.

Conclusion

In this final paragraph you tie all your ideas together by giving you own opinion and stating why you believe this. You need to refer back to the essay title/question to make sure you are giving a relevant answer. Your opinion should link to one of the points already discussed in the essay, don't suddenly include a completely new point which has not previously been discussed.

And you're done !!

Index

CPSIA information can be obtained
at www.ICGtesting.com
Printed in the USA
BVOW05s0951250817
492871BV00032B/256/P